Isaiah Berlin, in his famous essay, once divided
thinkers into two groups: hedgehogs, who know one
big thing, and foxes, who know many things. Proust
and Shakespeare. Separating writers into one camp
or another has long been a sport of undergraduate
humanities majors when the 2 a.m. pot of coffee
starts to kick in.

The food world has always had a weakness for people
who know one small thing - specialists. One of the
pleasures of travel is being able to stop by the
Singapore hawker stall whose family has been selling
the same kind of noodles for three generations, the
Umbrian stand that sells only porchetta, the South
Korean alley where nothing but boiled pig's feet are
sold. I still remember the astonishment, on my first
trip to Spain, of stumbling into a cafe that sold
nothing but toast. That toast, charcoal-broiled and
spread thickly with good butter, was magnificent.

I was thinking about that toast the other day
over breakfast at Sqirl, a sort-of cafe that
Jessica Koslow carved out of a tiny East Hollywood
storefront. Koslow, a former television producer,
has become well-known in the last couple of years
for her exquisite, expensive, small-batch jams,
made from local fruit and sold in handsome hand-
labeled jars. You seek out Koslow at the Altadena
farmers market because you never quite know when
her blueberry jam with thyme is going to be sold
out for the year or whether the Warren pear butter
will have just come in. She's pretty masterful at
capturing the specific nuances of fruit, sweetness
and dust (what winemakers call terroir), but the
unpredictability of supply is part of the fun.

Koslow is a micro-hedgehog: She captures the flavor
of a season and a place in a jar. Her cafe exists to
reanimate the flavors she preserves, to display them
as they ought to be displayed: rice porridge with
toasted hazelnuts and jam; rice tossed with tart
sorrel pesto and preserved lemon; fried eggs with
puréed tomatillos and house-fermented hot sauce,
just a smidge of hot sauce.

When I started thinking about that toast I'd eaten
in Madrid, I happened to be eating Koslow's toast,
a thick slice of brioche, crisp yet crumbly, spread
with a kind of mild chutney made from local Santa
Rosa plums, edge to edge, corner to corner, in a
layer much thicker than anyone would dare to put
down on his own. On top of the jam, like the Earth's
thin crust riding on its sea of magma, was a thin
layer of shaved pecorino from Bellwether Farms in
Sonoma, whose mellow, nutty funk sank into the tangy
jam, and above that was a single slice of cooked
bacon whose provenance I forgot to ask. (I could
have gotten a lightly fried duck egg for a buck more
if I had wanted one.)

I ate this toast outside in a sort of side yard
next to the restaurant, chased with sips of milky
espresso, in full earshot of the auto body shop up
the street and the banda music pounding from the
passing cars. It didn't just reflect a Silver Lake
afternoon; it was a Silver Lake afternoon.

-Jonathan Gold, Counter Intelligence, Dec. 5, 2012

The Sqirl Jam
(Jelly, Fruit Butter, and Others) Book

Dedicated to Ryan Erlich, Scott Barry, David Prado, and the entire Sqirl crew, past and present, who believe in the power of fruit preservation. And to you, dear readers, for marking a moment in time by . . . squirreling it away for later.

The Sqirl Jam
(Jelly, Fruit Butter, and Others) Book

Jessica Koslow
With Betty Hallock

Photography by Scott Barry

ABRAMS, NEW YORK

Persian mulberry jam page 68

Table of Contents

Introduction

Jam is the Sqirl creation story. Now an internationally recognized breakfast-and-lunch restaurant on the East Hollywood corner of Virgil and Marathon Streets, Sqirl started as a tiny jam company. And everything since then has radiated from our jam-making genesis.

It's a holistic part of everything we do every day. Our trips to the farmers' markets revolve around finding what fruit is in season. Or farmers know to call us when a particular fruit is available, and the entire staff experiences the frisson of coming Persian mulberries or Mara des Bois—for turning into jam. We dubbed our main storage area Jam World because of all the fruit and preserves kept there.

Why jam? The idea came as a light-bulb moment—a moment that was nearly two decades in the making.

In 2005, I worked as a pastry cook at Bacchanalia in Atlanta and watched the farmers coming through the kitchen's back door hauling in all of their produce. This was a restaurant in the South, so it was our job to preserve everything, because the quantities were small and the seasons were fleeting. "Putting up" was just the southern way.

When I eventually returned to Los Angeles and its farmers' markets, it was more apparent than ever that I'd been taking so much year-round abundance for granted. I saw these things that we had so much of, for so much of the year, and it was such great product. I thought, We should be canning all this.

I had to leave L.A., live in Boston and D.C. and New York, cook in the South, and finally return to California to realize exactly what I wanted to do. I gave my life over to jam.

Sqirl started soon after I met Scott Barry, now a partner and the company's creative director. I'm the inside of the jar; he's the outside of the jar. We wanted to figure out how to combine our perspectives. How do you put that in a jar and make it something everyone wants to eat? I wanted to call it Squirrel, for squirreling away. Scott hated the word, especially design-wise, and landed on "Sqirl."

What's inside a jar of Sqirl jam is not the jam you get at the grocery store. That stuff has added pectin, which means you need more sugar, which means the flavor of the fruit is muted. The fruit itself is frozen or out of season or from somewhere else in the country or world. The texture is a monotonous gel. It has tainted our palates. We've accepted subpar jam for too long.

What I know as jam is made with in-season, of-the-moment fruit and its own natural pectin in small batches in copper pots. In 2012, Sqirl made five thousand jars of jam. Now that number is more than thirty-five thousand jars a year, still made by hand in copper pots. On top of that we make buckets of it for service—ten thousand gallons a year for the ricotta toast alone. Jam is the heart and soul of everything we do.

It connects us to the seasons, to the farmers—experiencing what they have to offer every week. You can't do that making a huge industrial-vat-size portion of jam all at once. The seasonality of what we do means we have

Opposite: Gravenstein apple butter. Above (clockwise from bottom left): Loquat jam, tomato jam with caraway, apple pectin, and the jam of a friend.

Santa Rosa plum jam (page 108) on toast

to work within ourselves, to follow the market, to stay honest. There's integrity to the product that we're using and the product we're making.

What works for us here at Sqirl works at home, too. We built an entire business around the best-quality jams we could produce. And the great thing is that it makes sense for several reasons: Jam isn't that hard to make, a little goes a long way, and it has an extended shelf life. Long live jam.

What I'm talking about when I talk about jam is fruit, sugar, and acid (like the citric acid in lemon juice), brought to a certain temperature so that it gels to become some sort of fruit spread. Are we at a point in 2020 where we can use the blanket word jam to mean jellies, marmalades, butters, fruit spreads, and other preserves? I'm going to say yes. A lot of the technical terminology tends to overlap anyway.

Sqirl's jams are technically fruit spreads, lower in sugar, and with a specific texture that's both lush and easy to spread. It's something that we developed over time so that it went with our food—not just according to how it spreads, but also how it interacts with ricotta, how it pairs with nut butters, how it stands on its own.

Sqirl jam is a philosophy. I'm looking for the right balance between sweetness and acidity and the flavor of the fruit. It's important to pick fruit that can show its quality in the jam. (That's why I love Mara des Bois strawberries, which taste like the essence of the fruit. It's also why I struggle with some varieties of stone fruit, because there's so much sweetness in them.) The flavor needs to withstand the temperature—up to around 221°F—necessary to take it to jam. My job is to keep the nuance of the fruit alive.

I used to be a competitive figure skater, when "school figures"—intricate patterns that skaters traced on the ice to demonstrate their skill in making clean turns—were part of the sport. It was quiet, sensitive, exacting, and really challenging. It was not exciting. There were no sparkles, no music. Competitions could take up to six hours. Jam is like school figures. There's something sensual about it. It's almost like I traded my feet for my hands.

Being a jam maker doesn't hold a candle to being a Michelin-starred chef. It doesn't have the same glitz and glamour. There are few people who pronounce, "I'm going to be the world's greatest jam maker."

But to me, it became something I really love to do because of the dance of it, the same gratification of executing something correctly over and over, and the discovery of luster in that. Hundreds of thousands of jars of jam later, I still feel the same way.

I Don't Eat Fruit
an Interview with Mom

Surprise! I used to only like fruit in jam form.
Just ask my mom.

JESSICA Do you remember trying to feed me fruit?

MOM The only flavor of baby food that you would eat was vanilla rhubarb. Everything else you would spit into my face. It was a pudding. Gerbers made a vanilla rhubarb pudding.

JESSICA That's kind of cool, because the rhubarb is kind of acidic . . . I'm assuming there's not sugar in the rhubarb. Is it weird that I want to try that now?

MOM Everything else got spit back in my face. You ate very little. You were finicky from the get-go on food.

JESSICA Which is weird, because I'm so not finicky now.

MOM That's why I took you to farmers' markets to try to get you to eat fruit. To get you to see that people were actually involved in bringing these things to market. We used to go to Dooley's in Long Beach. Farmers' markets then weren't a big deal, just the farmers coming

to a big parking lot. I used to drive you there every Sunday, and I'd say, "Okay, let's try something." And when other people got involved, you'd start trying things. So if a farmer gave you something, you'd try it.

JESSICA Really? Because my memory is that I just wouldn't try it.

MOM You would try it from the farmer and smile and then throw it out when we walked away. When it comes to food at home, anything that was a fruit you just would not eat. Except raspberries. I thought watermelon, all kids like watermelon, but no.

JESSICA This past Rosh Hashanah we had apples over honey at Becca's house. I feel that was the first time I had apples and honey. It was the first time I actively pursued eating it as a part of the day. You know, I was like, "Okay, I'm going to do this," as a ritual, apples and honey. I remember being at the JCC and it was time for apples and honey and I just wouldn't do it.

MOM You would just put your foot down, put your arms across your chest, tap your toe, and shake your head.

JESSICA I guess my question is, do you remember trying to feed me . . . well, bananas?

MOM [Shaking her head.] I tried oranges. [Shakes her head.] The minute you tried raspberries, you said you'd eat raspberries and that was it. That's where we started and ended. They weren't always in season. I tried blackberries, blueberries, all the melons, watermelon, cantaloupe.

JESSICA Honestly, melon is still something I can't eat. I can't really do melon. Actually, the two things I'm challenged by are bananas and melons, like musk melons, anything that's really smelly like that. And hilariously, it's something you can't really can. You can make a jelly out of it, but you can't really make a jam out of it. And so the musk melons, any melon, and bananas I still can't really do.

MOM I don't really eat bananas and I can't stand citrus. But I tried giving you oranges. I tried everything. We had pomegranates and you would eat those. We had them in the backyard and you'd eat a few of those seeds because they were fun.

JESSICA I do really miss having a pomegranate tree. I do love pomegranates.

MOM Raspberry and pomegranate, that was it. I tried kiwi, I tried everything.

JESSICA Was there a moment you remember giving me jam?

MOM No. I was so thin at that point in my life. And I didn't want to introduce sugar.

JESSICA Right. Totally, that was the thing. There was no sugar. I remember carrots. Black licorice. It made me a sugar fiend. I was a fiend for candy. Now I can't. If I drink a glass of wine and have birthday cake at a party, I get a migraine. So did you eat a lot of fruit? I remember a lot of stone fruit.

MOM Tons. We had plums, we had nectarines, we had cherries, every berry I could lay my hands on. We had tons of melons. I mean, I love fresh fruit. Of course, when you raise a child you expect they're going to be somewhat like you. You wouldn't eat any of it.

JESSICA Were you burned out by trying to feed me?

MOM It was so frustrating. I could not understand. It was so difficult to get you to eat anything. You were so skinny. You would push everything around on the plate. I really was worried about you in terms of malnutrition. You liked what you liked and that was it. We loaded you up with what you could eat.

JESSICA I'm fine, I turned out fine. I was probably full of apple fritters and candy. Will you tell the story of the tomatoes? I find it to be very funny.

MOM I developed a theory that if she helped me grow it, she'd eat it.

JESSICA It was a good plot—well, not a plot, but two hundred square feet.

MOM I tried growing all kinds of things. You can pretty successfully grow tomatoes. I knew you didn't like tomatoes, but I thought cherry tomatoes might work, because they're small and they're kind of fun. I turned to you and said, "We're going to try cherry tomatoes, we're going to plant baby tomatoes." You were still a toddler. The next thing I know, you come out of the kitchen with a box of cherry tomatoes from the refrigerator and start planting them in the ground. That was as close as you got to eating a tomato.

JESSICA It was a texture thing. Like biting into it and getting that explosion. I mean, it still bothers me even if I eat fruit. I don't just go to eat an apple. I'll eat vegetables all day long. But fruit is something I cut into very small pieces in order to taste. It's more for taste than anything else. When did I first eat jam?

MOM We used to go to Knott's Berry Farm. We would go there just to eat the fried chicken. They had rhubarb, first of all. It was a sauce. You could have it with your biscuits or your fried chicken. Just like the pickles. You had to know to order it.

JESSICA And jam. That was my first iconic memory of jam, really looking forward to that flavor. The thing that was offered to me I didn't want. The thing that I wanted wasn't in the house.

MOM It was not in my taste buds. Why would I bring sugar to the household in the eighties? Are you kidding me? I think I did get some Knott's Berry Farm jams when we were there, to bring home, and we would have them with peanut butter, and that was about it. It's interesting because my father's mother canned and preserved everything. I grew up with jam everywhere in the house. Maybe because it was there I didn't eat it.

JESSICA You should talk about that. Your grandma worked in a canning factory.

MOM When she was fifteen. When she came to the United States from Russia by herself. And at home they preserved everything. She canned morning, noon, and night. Preservation of vegetables, of fruits, everything. And she made jams. They were wonderful. I guess I took it for granted that that's what people did. I was never good at any of that, so I didn't do it. It never dawned on me at all. It must have skipped a couple of generations.

Canning Tools

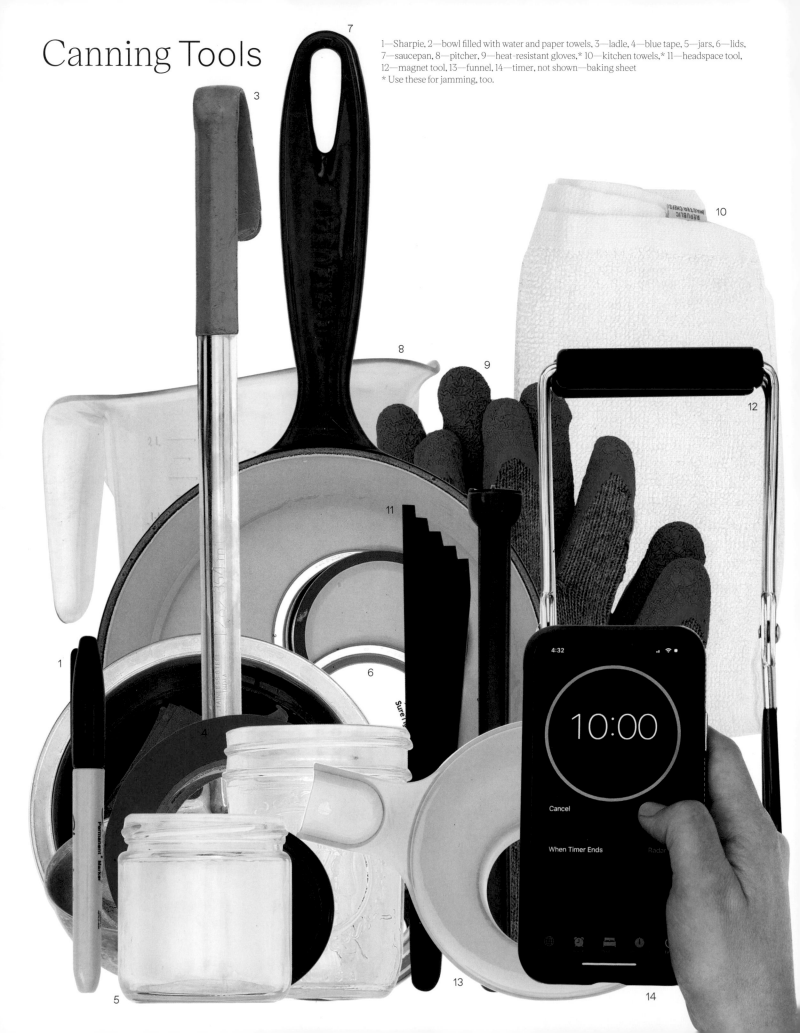

1—Sharpie, 2—bowl filled with water and paper towels, 3—ladle, 4—blue tape, 5—jars, 6—lids, 7—saucepan, 8—pitcher, 9—heat-resistant gloves,* 10—kitchen towels,* 11—headspace tool, 12—magnet tool, 13—funnel, 14—timer, not shown—baking sheet
* Use these for jamming, too.

Jamming Tools

1—thermometer, 2—cheesecloth (we use a reusable Norpro turkey stuffing bag), 3—long-handled high-heat spatula, 4—knife, 5—scale, 6—cutting board, 7—8-quart enameled pot, 8—food processor, 9—fine-mesh skimmer, not shown—mixing bowls (and your hands—your best tool)

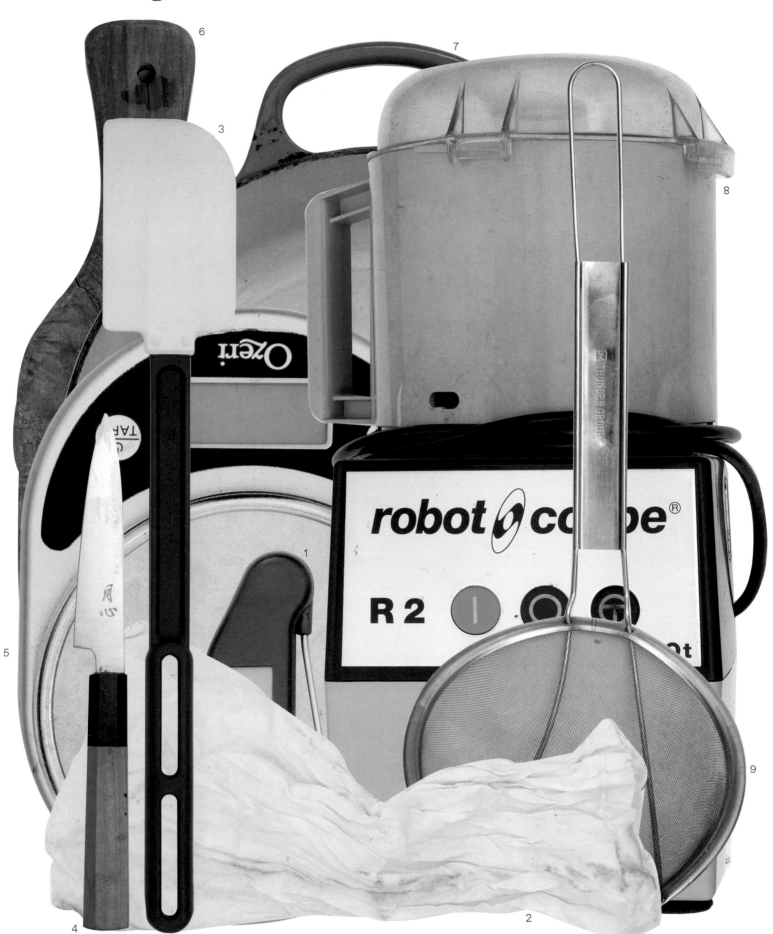

The Sqirl Way

Fruit

The state of your fruit matters. It should be ripe. Stone fruit needs to be fully soft. Pears and apples and quince need to be soft too. Process fruit at its peak. Berries such as strawberries, cherries—anything that tends to dissolve quickly, whether berries or Blenheim apricots or juicy plums or Gravenstein apples or for god's sake Persian mulberries—you've got to can immediately. This will provide optimal pectin content. Besides, you don't want your fruit sitting around for too long. Anything that can turn quickly should be canned quickly, not only so that it doesn't ferment but also to retain the essence of the fruit.

We buy varieties of fruit grown within 350 miles. There are a few exceptions—when someone gives me Marionberries while I'm visiting Oregon, or brings me cranberries from a friend's cranberry bog. But local fruit dictates the majority of our offerings and the majority of the recipes in this book. This is all to say, find your local. The recipe will indeed work—and perhaps you'll find the desire to tweak the ratios to make it your own.

If you're at the farmers' market and tasting fruit and it's really, really sweet, I wouldn't buy it other than for as-is consumption. Fruit, especially stone fruit, needs to have high acid to counterbalance the sugar in your jam. Except for Greengage plums and Mirabelles. They're just sugar fairies and that's what they're meant to be. But in general, find fruit that has high acidity so that your jam is balanced.

Ratios

A jam is a living being; it's in flux. Sometimes it won't be sweet enough, or it will be too sweet and you adjust by reducing the sugar and/or increasing the acid. This can change from season to season, from week to week, or even from batch to batch. The important thing to know is that it's always a ratio of fruit, sugar, and acid. (My favorite economics teacher in college, Dr. Chad Bowne, would hit me over the head with the idea that there's a perfect intersection of supply and demand—same goes here for fruit, sugar, and acid. There's a happy intersection that keeps the jam fruit-forward, safe enough to be preserved, and perfect in texture.) Percentages of these three main ingredients are provided in most of the recipes, as well as formulas for making adjustments if you don't happen to have, say, five pounds of blueberries for blueberry tarragon jam. These may look scary or complicated, but they're empowering. It's almost like not needing a recipe at all.

Blending and Plumping

The texture of Sqirl's jams is a big part of what makes them Sqirl. In general, we're looking for continuity, a homogeneity of fruit and sugar—but with some latitude. We're not inflexible. There are a couple of ways we approach texture. Most of the time the fruit is pureed. At Sqirl we accomplish that in a way that's #NSFH (not safe for home). So for many of the recipes in this book, the fruit is blended before cooking. The resulting texture is a fruit spread that's like wearing a cashmere tracksuit: luxurious but not too refined. This texture of Sqirl jam did not start out like this. It evolved, over time, due to the need to spread the jam on our ricotta (toast).

Our jam started out more in line with the approach that highlights texture through our technique of plumping. And honestly, if I make jam at home, I tend to go this route. Why? I want texture. I want to taste the segments of fruit. But this can lead to seepage and also be a challenge to spread smoothly on ricotta. Okay—back to the question, what is "plumping"?

This is the term we use for letting the fruit (whether it's intact or crushed or pureed) sit in the sugar and lemon juice for hours or days before cooking. Step 1: Combine the fruit, sugar, and lemon juice in a large bowl. Cover the mixture with parchment paper or plastic wrap, directly touching the fruit, and let sit for 3 to 4 hours or overnight in the refrigerator. Step 2: Transfer the mixture to your jamming pot and bring it to a boil. Immediately remove from the heat and let cool. Transfer to a heatproof (such as Pyrex) container and let cool. Cover. Let the mixture rest again for 3 to 4 hours, or overnight in the refrigerator. Step 3: Put the mixture in your jamming pot and bring to a boil. Proceed with the rest of your recipe, cooking the fruit until it's jam.

Plumping pulls out a lot of the moisture (this means less foaming) and allows the fruit to absorb as much sugar as possible, so it's better prepared to withstand the cooking temperatures and times that jam requires. This is a good technique when you want a chunkier jam, or bigger fruit pieces suspended in fruit gel. Or you could blend half your fruit and leave the other half whole, and you'll get a beautiful jam—low-pectin-content fruits like figs, strawberries, and blueberries—and just stone fruit and berries in general.

Lazy Jam? I've determined that there's also an even lazier way to go about the plumping technique. The resulting texture is not as luscious or silky but is very similar: adding the sugar and jam—letting it macerate and then popping it in the fridge for two to three days. (I've heard whispers that you could leave it in the fridge for up to 5 days. This, I haven't tried.)

Sugar

Technically, a majority of Sqirl jams are considered fruit spreads—a jam containing less than 65 percent sugar. We use a lot less sugar than in the stuff you'd find on your grocery store shelf. In general, it's a lot less sugar than fruit by weight. The amount of sugar used is always in flux depending on the fruit and its sugar content. Peaches have a high natural sugar content, and we account for that to get the right flavor balance. Note that sugar is one of the things that preserves jams. The more sugar, the more shelf stable. The less sugar we add, the less shelf stable it is. (I find peaches and apricots to mold the fastest . . . so use these jams first!) Sqirl jams that have been properly canned will keep for 15 to 20 months in the cupboard (other jams might might keep for 24 months). Once opened, store the jam in the refrigerator for up to another several months, or until it sadly molds.

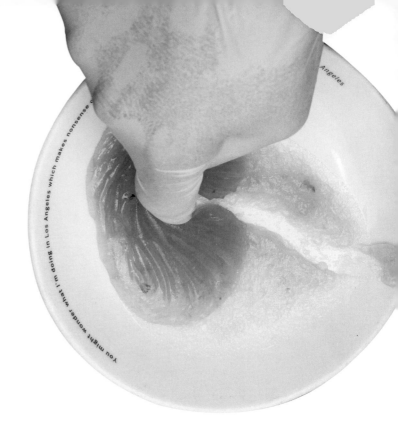

Stirring

If you're making jam, you know you're in for some stirring. You have to stir so that the sugar in your jam doesn't caramelize. This will diminish any fruit flavor. While you're stirring, you're scraping the bottom of the pot with your heatproof spatula. Stir, pushing away from your chest, back and forth and around the bottom of the pot. But don't scrape the sides. As the jam reduces, you don't want to be pushing junk that builds up on the sides back into the pot.

Temperatures and times

Jelly and marmalade set at 221°F (105°C). That's a gel set—gel is the stuff around the fruit in, for example, a marmalade. With jam, you're not looking for a gel set, you're looking for what I call a "fruit set." It can be hard to be precise. The final temperature isn't something set in stone. You're going to start to get a feel for exactly what texture you want. For non-jellies/marmalades our range is 214°F to 218°F (101°C to 103°C), depending on the ratios of fruit to sugar. When you turn the heat off, it's cooling at a very rapid rate. So get busy canning right away. You don't want to lose a lot of heat. I always say making jam is best to do with a companion, because quick work is quicker with two. (For example, one person can pour the jam while the other person cleans the rim and seals the jar with a lid.) Approximate times are provided in the recipes, but every stove is different so it might take more or less time to reach the temperature.

Testing

The plate test is the most reliable. Just start testing a few degrees before the final temperature. If you've gone too far, there's no turning back. But if the jam is still too loose, you can always put it back on the heat for another minute or two and test again. Almost all of the recipes start with: "Prepare your plate test by putting a few saucers in the freezer." A frozen plate will show whether or not your jam is set when a little of the jam is spooned onto it. After a couple of minutes back in the freezer, when you run your finger through the jam, you should see a strip of clean plate. Now you're ready to can (or to not can, which is also an option).

See pages 16–21 for Sqirling away your jam.

The Sqirl Way

Step-by-Step Canning

The Sqirl Way of canning—using lug-lid jars and putting them into the oven—allows us to process a lot of jam at once. It's canning in a professional setting, where it's done very quickly with the help of more than one person, and isn't necessarily the best option for home cooks. Water-bath canning is the most widely used method for home jammers. We outline both methods here. There is also the option of not canning at all: Transfer your jam to any jar or covered container and keep it in the refrigerator for anywhere from a few weeks to months, depending on the jam (you'll know to toss it when you see mold).

Stovetop Method: Water Bath Canning

1. Heat your jars before you start making jam. Prepare a water bath (such as from a canning kit) fitted with a rack on the stove. Place the jars in sideways so that they fill with water before setting them right-side up. Meanwhile, put the lids in a 2-quart pot of water over low heat.

2. Using tongs, remove the jars from the water bath, by first lifting straight up and then turning the jar sideways, pouring the water out of each jar into the pot. Set the jars on clean towels.

3. After you make your jam, ladle it into a heatproof pitcher.

4. Pour the jam into each jar, using a funnel, leaving ¼ inch of space in each jar. (If you've overfilled, spoon some into the next jar. If you have any leftover jam that won't fill a full jar, store it in the refrigerator and use for up to several weeks.)

Stovetop method: Water Bath Canning

5. Wipe the rims with paper towels.

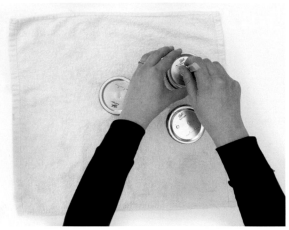

6. Use the magnet tool to remove the lids from their pot of water and place them on the jars. Holding the lid on the sides to keep it in place on the jar, remove the magnet tool.

7. Take the rings from a bowl and screw them on, not too tight and not too loose, so that there is a little space for air to shift.

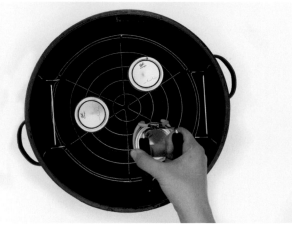

8. Using the tongs, put the jars back into the water bath, right-side up (straight down), and bring it to a boil.

9. Set a timer for 10 minutes; once the timer goes off, turn off the heat and set the timer for another 10 minutes.

10. Using the tongs, grab the jars from the top (there's a ridge near the top of the jar) and lift them straight up from the water to towels on the counter. Let them sit undisturbed overnight. You should hear them pop as they seal. In the morning you'll know whether they sealed properly. If a jar doesn't seal, put it in the fridge; it will keep for up to several weeks.

11. Label the jars with the name of the jam and date. These will keep in a cool, dry place for about 2 years.

*For more information about water bath canning, refer to the USDA's Complete Guide to Home Canning, which is available online.

Oven method: Lug-lid Canning

1. Sterilize your jars before you start making jam: Heat the oven to 225°F (107°C). Put the lids in a bowl and set aside. Put the jars on a baking sheet and put them in the oven while you're preparing your jam (or for at least 15 minutes). Remove the sheet tray from the oven only when you are ready to can. (Keep the oven on at 225°F [107°C].)

2. Ladle the hot cooked jam into a heatproof pitcher.

3. Pour the jam into the prepared jars, using a funnel if you'd like, leaving ¼ inch of space in each jar. Work quickly so that the jam doesn't cool down too much. (If you've overfilled, spoon some into the next jar. If you have any leftover jam that won't fill a full jar, store it in the refrigerator and use for up to several weeks.)

4. Use paper towels to wipe the rims of the jars clean. We're using our bare hands because we work fast. But the jars are hot! Wear gloves if you can't handle the heat.

5. Wearing gloves (I use latex-coated gardening gloves), put the lids on the jars. I like to turn to the left first and then to the right, until the lid feels locked, like you can't turn it anymore—but not too tight, or the lid will strip and won't lock—you'll get a feel for it. I highly suggest "going too far" with a lid, so you know what going too far feels like! (The work goes by that much faster if you have help—one person to fill and clean the jars, the other person to put on the lids.)

6. Flip the jars upside-down onto your baking sheet. Once you've filled all of the jars, keep them upside-down for 2 to 3 minutes. Then flip them again so they're right-side up on the baking sheet.

7. Put the baking sheet of jars in the oven for about 25 minutes. You want the interior of the jam to be 185°F (85°C). One of your jars will have to be a martyr; open it up, put your thermometer in it, and if it isn't 185°F (85°C), return the jars to the oven. Use the martyr to retest.

8. Remove the jars from the oven. Let them sit out overnight and check the seals in the morning. If a seal has popped, put the jar in the refrigerator; it will keep for up to several weeks. Label the jars with the name of the jam and date. These will keep in your pantry for about 15 months.

*This is how we can at Sqirl. It isn't necessarily ideal for home cooks. It's important to check that the jam has reached 185°F (85°C). The jars must be sealed tightly so as not to let in air. If you do use lug lids, get the ones with the button.

Step-by-Step Canning

Jam Glossary

Jam Glossary

The full rainbow of jams is a spectrum of color and texture, each one representing its moment in the season. This glossary shows what our jams look like when fully set and cooled, not what they look like directly out of the pot.

Jam Glossary: Berries

Raspberry jam with vanilla [40]

Blueberry jam with tarragon [42]

Black and blue [45]

Blackberry–Meyer lemon jam [46]

Boysenberry jam [48]

Berries

Boysenberry-apricot jam [51]

Tayberry jam [56]

Classic strawberry jam [58]

Mara des Bois strawberry jam [60]

Pakistan mulberry jam [66]

Persian mulberry jam [68]

Rhubarb

Rhubarb jam [76]

Raspberry-rhubarb jam [78]

Blueberry-rhubarb jam [80]

Strawberry-rhubarb jam [82]

Rhubarb-kumquat jam [84]

Stone Fruit

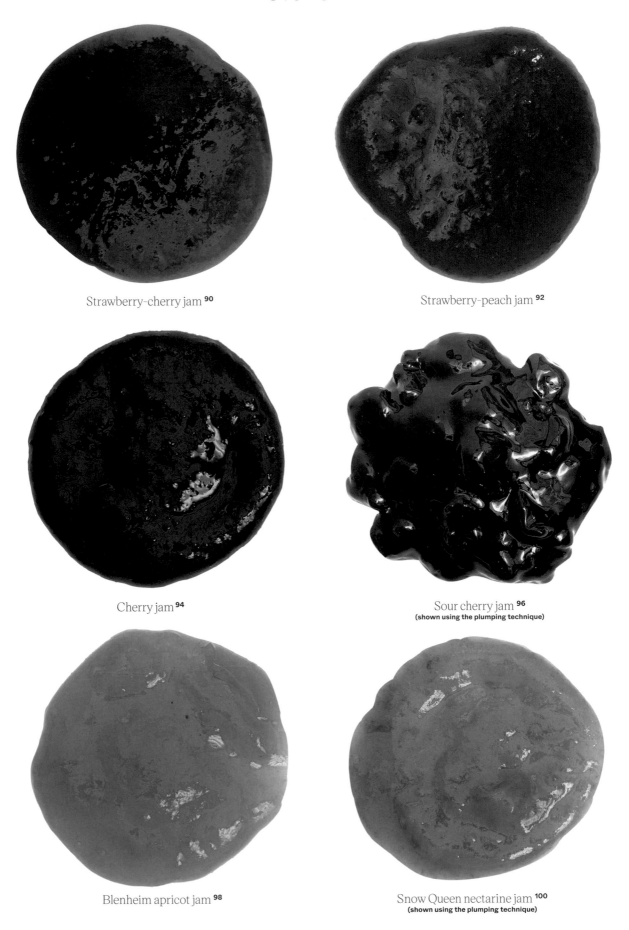

Strawberry-cherry jam **90**

Strawberry-peach jam **92**

Cherry jam **94**

Sour cherry jam **96**
(shown using the plumping technique)

Blenheim apricot jam **98**

Snow Queen nectarine jam **100**
(shown using the plumping technique)

Stone Fruit

June and Rich Lady peach jam **104**

Elephant Heart plum jam **106**

Santa Rosa plum jam with flowering thyme **108**

Mirabelle plum jam **112**

Damson plum cheese **114**

Honey Punch pluot jam **122**

Stone Fruit

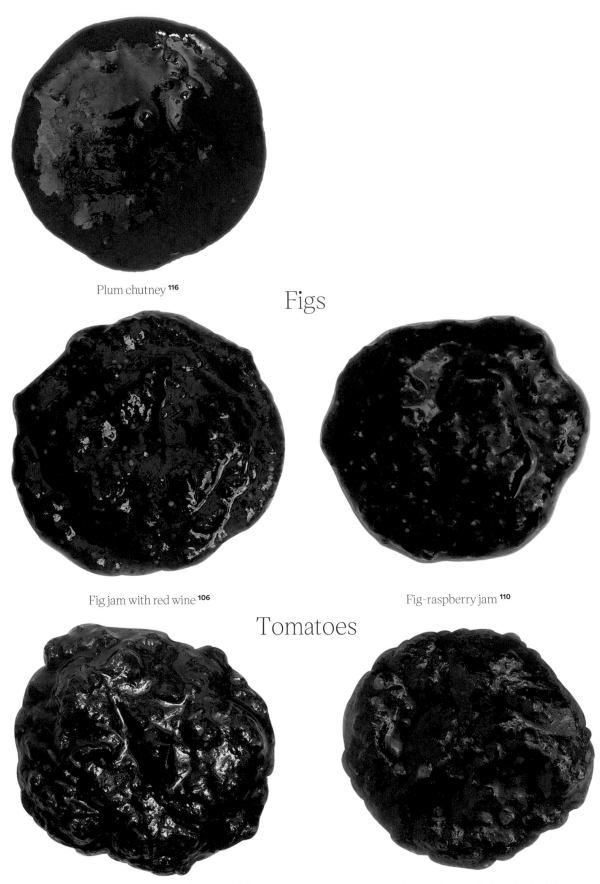

Plum chutney [116]

Figs

Fig jam with red wine [106]

Fig-raspberry jam [110]

Tomatoes

Tomato jam with saffron and caraway [138]

Tomato jam with tamarind and mint [140]
(shown with optional chile)

Tropical Fruits

Mango–passion fruit jam **146**

Guava jam **148**

Medlars

Medlar butter **152**

Loquat butter **154**

Quince membrillo **204**

(Sorry this is out of order. We ran out of room on the quince page.)

Apples, Pears, Quince, Persimmons & Pomegranates

Gravenstein apple butter [174]

Roasted honey apple butter [176]

Blackberry-apple butter [182]

Apple jelly [180]

Passion fruit–apple jelly [184]

Pomegranate-apple jelly [186]

Apples, Pears, Quince, Persimmons & Pomegranates

Pomegranate-persimmon butter [188]

Warren pear butter [194]

Quince-raspberry butter [196]

Quince butter with rosemary [198]

Quince jelly [202]

Fuyu persimmon butter [206]

Cranberries & Grapes

Bourbon cranberry jam [158]

Cranberry-apple butter [160]

Concord grape jam [162]

Scuppernong jam [166]

Citrus

Blood orange marmalade with vanilla bean [212]

Blood orange jelly with Campari [216]

Citrus

Cara Cara orange–Meyer lemon–fennel marmalade [218]

Cara Cara orange marmalade with hibiscus [220]

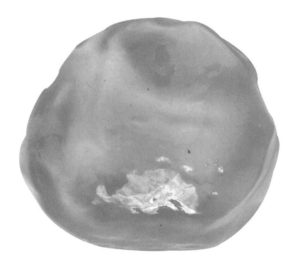

Seville orange jelly [226]

Seville orange marmalade [228]

Bergamot buckwheat marmalade [230]

Lemon-lime shred [232]

Citrus

Kumquat marmalade with chamomile [236]

Kumquat-mandarinquat-limequat marmalade [238]

Rangpur lime–mandarin marmalade [240]

Yuzu marmalade with honey [242]

Meyer lemon–kiwi marmalade [244]

Retracing Erwin Wurm with lemons, downtown Los Angeles.

Citrus season at the Santa Monica Farmers Market.

BERRIES
40–73

Berries

Raspberry jam with vanilla[40], Blueberry jam with tarragon[42], Black and blue[45], Blackberry–Meyer lemon jam[46], Boysenberry–apricot jam[48] The tayberry incident[52] Tayberry jam[52] Classic strawberry jam[58] Mara des Bois strawberry jam[60] Fumio makes jam[62] Pakistan mulberry jam[66] Persian mulberry jam[68] Brown butter blondies[70] Linzer torte[72]

Raspberries were the only fruit I would eat as a child. So of course I'm going to make raspberry jam. And the kid in me would add vanilla, so that's in here too.

Raspberry jam with vanilla Berries

Makes 8 half-pint jars

INGREDIENTS

2,000 g (4 lb 6 oz)	**raspberries**
1,200 g (6 cups)	**sugar** (60% of the weight of raspberries)
60 g (¼ cup)	**lemon juice** (3% of the weight of raspberries)
½	**vanilla pod, seeds scraped**

Prepare your plate test by putting a few saucers in the freezer.

If you have more or less than 2,000 g raspberries, you can figure out how much sugar and lemon juice you need by using the following formula:

Grams of raspberries × 0.60 = grams of sugar
Grams of raspberries × 0.03 = grams of lemon juice

Put the raspberries in a food processor and pulse until they are chopped but still a little chunky. (Alternatively, you can put the berries in a large bowl and crush them with your hands. Or for a mix of textures, puree half the berries in the food processor and squeeze the other half with your hands.)

Transfer the berries to a large bowl and stir in the sugar and lemon juice; let sit for at least a few minutes or up to 30 minutes if you have the time. (You also have the option to use the plumping technique here; see "Blending and Plumping" on page 14.)

Pour the mixture into your jamming pot.

Cook over high heat, stirring and scraping the bottom of the pot so the sugars don't burn. Use a spider or fine-mesh skimmer to skim off any scum. (There won't be a lot, but there'll be some.) Dip the spider into a bowl of water and shake off any excess to clean between skims. If the jam is bubbling more than you can manage, it's okay to turn off the heat, skim, then turn the heat back on.

As the jam cooks, the solids will separate from the liquid and then rejoin. You'll see the surface will look matte at the beginning, then it will suddenly change to shiny and glossy. Sometimes with raspberry jam, the surface will form what look like dry patches. This indicates that the jam is nearly done. It usually takes 10 to 12 minutes and the temperature will reach about 217°F (103°C) when done. When the jam nears this temperature, remove from the heat and stir in the scraped vanilla pod and seeds. This is a good time for a plate test.

Spoon a little bit of the jam onto a frozen saucer. Put the plate back in the freezer for 1 minute, then slide a finger through the jam. It's done when it parts and you see a strip of clean saucer. If it isn't set, return the pot to the heat, stir frequently, and test after another minute. Before you jar the jam, remove the vanilla pod with tongs and discard.

To Sqirl away your jam, see pages 16–21.

Variation:
Raspberry jam with cardamom

You can find the recipe for raspberry cardamom jam on page 192 in *Everything I Want to Eat: Sqirl and the New California Cooking.*

BLUEBERRY JAM WITH TARRAGON

To me, grapes and tarragon make the most beautiful marriage. And blueberries are the grapes of berries, right? Blending the blueberries helps to draw out the pectin and make a cohesive jam. You can make this without blending; just know that you'll be smashing them the whole time to amalgamate the berries with the sugar, and the jam—which is actually more like what I think of as "preserves"—will seep liquid. Which is totally okay.

Makes 8 half-pint jars

INGREDIENTS

2,300 g (5 lb 1 oz)	**blueberries**
1,380 g (6¾ cups plus 2½ Tbsp)	**sugar** (60% of the weight of blueberries)
46 g (3 Tbsp)	**lemon juice** (2% of the weight of blueberries), plus the lemon rinds
9 g (a few)	**fresh tarragon sprigs**

Prepare your plate test by putting a few saucers in the freezer.

If you have more or less than 2,300 g blueberries, you can figure out how much sugar and lemon juice you need by using the following formula:

Grams of blueberries × 0.60 = grams of sugar
Grams of blueberries × 0.02 = grams of lemon juice

Combine the blueberries, sugar, and lemon juice in a large bowl. Put the mixture in a blender and blend until smooth. (Alternatively, you can put the berries in a large bowl and crush them with your hands. Or for a mix of textures, puree half the berries in the food processor or blender and squeeze the other half with your hands.) Pour the puree back into the bowl and let sit overnight. (You also have the option to use the plumping technique here; see "Blending and Plumping" on page 14.)

Transfer the puree to a jamming pot. Put the tarragon and lemon rinds in a cheesecloth sachet tied with kitchen string and add it to the blueberry mixture.

Cook over high heat, stirring occasionally. After about 15 minutes, reduce the heat to medium and using a spider or fine-mesh skimmer, start skimming scum that rises to the top. Dip the spider into a bowl of water and shake off any excess to clean between skims.

Continue to stir and skim. Cook until the jam thickens and is reduced by about half, and the temperature reaches 217°F (103°C), about 25 minutes total. When it nears this temperature, remove the pot from the heat. Remove the bag of tarragon and lemon rinds with tongs, squeezing any excess liquid into the pot, and discard. Give your jam a stir. This is a good time for a plate test.

Spoon a little of the jam onto a frozen saucer. Put the plate back in the freezer for 1 minute, then slide a finger through the jam. It's done when it parts and you see a strip of clean saucer. If it isn't set, return the pot to the heat, stir constantly, and test again after 1 to 2 minutes.

To Sqirl away your jam, see pages 16–21.

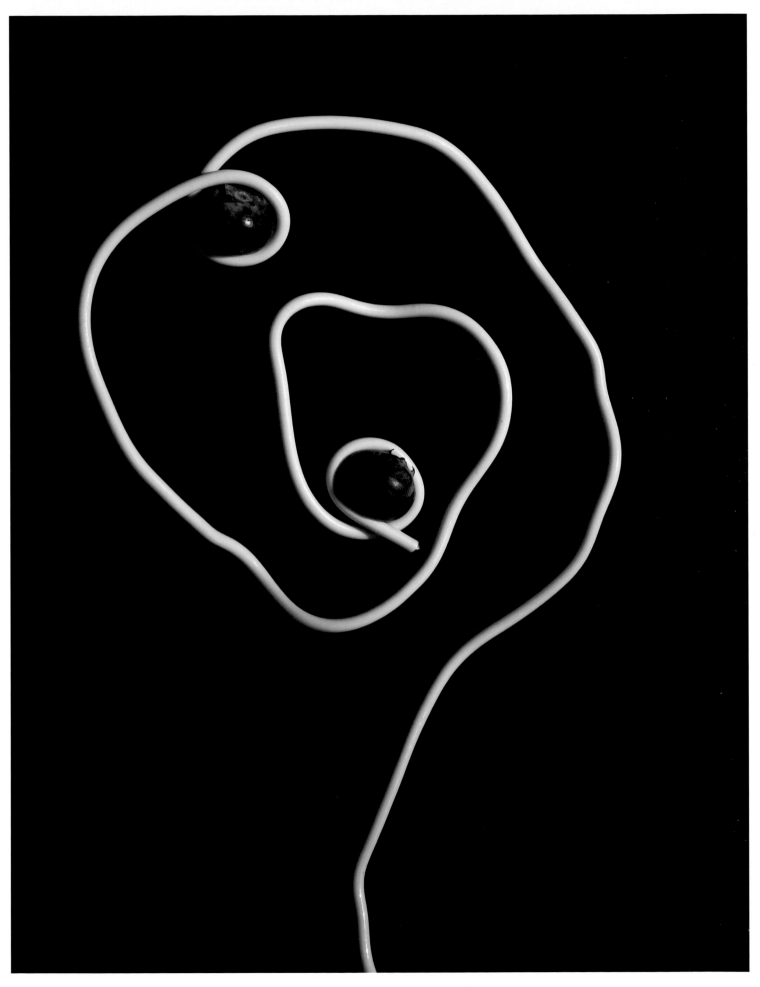

Blueberry jam with tarragon Berries

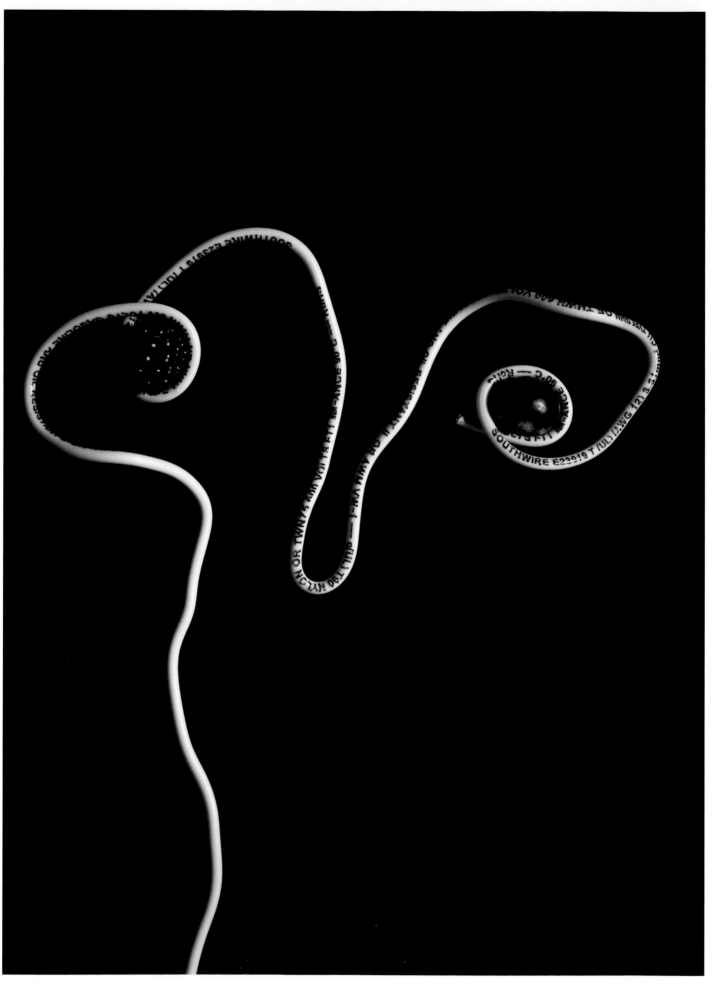

Black and blue Berries

BLACK AND BLUE

We use a mixture of a little more blackberries by weight than blueberries (60% blackberries to 40% blueberries), so it's more black than blue. With raspberries, mulberries, and blackberries, they do this thing, in jam mode, where they've reduced by about a third to a half when they're done. These berry jams have pockets of what look like the La Brea Tar Pits as they're cooking—dry, waxy sections on top of the jam. If you want a fruity texture, you don't have to blend the blueberries.

Makes 8 half-pint jars

INGREDIENTS

1,200 g (2 lb 10 oz)	**blackberries**
800 g (1 lb 12 oz)	**blueberries**
1,200 g (6 cups)	**sugar** (60% of the weight of blackberries plus blueberries)
40 g (2 Tbsp plus 2 tsp)	**lemon juice** (2% of the weight of blackberries plus blueberries), plus the lemon rinds

Prepare your plate test by putting a few saucers in the freezer.

If you have more or less than 1,200 g blackberries and 800 g blueberries (60% blackberries and 40% blueberries), you can figure out how much sugar and lemon juice you need by using the following formula:

Grams of blackberries plus blueberries × 0.60 = grams of sugar
Grams of blackberries plus blueberries × 0.02 = grams of lemon juice

Puree the blackberries and blueberries in a blender. (Alternatively, you can put the berries in a large bowl and crush them with your hands. Or for a mix of textures, puree half the berries in the food processor or blender and squeeze the other half with your hands.) Combine the berry puree, sugar, and lemon juice in a jamming pot. (Or, you also have the option to use the plumping technique here; see "Blending and Plumping" on page 14.) Put the lemon rinds in a cheesecloth sachet tied with kitchen string and drop that in the pot.

Cook over high heat, stirring often and scraping the bottom of the pot so the sugars don't burn. Use a spider or fine-mesh skimmer to skim off any scum that forms on the surface of the jam. Dip the spider into a bowl of water and shake off the excess to clean between skims.

Cook until the jam is glossy and thickened, reduced by about a third, and the temperature reaches about 217°F (103°C), about 15 minutes. It will look thick, but not too thick. It's a tricky balance because there are moments when it feels too loose. But if it looks "done" while still on the stove, you've gone too far. You have to think about how it's going to continue to congeal in the refrigerator. Too stiff a jam and you won't be able to spread it easily.

When the jam nears 217°F (103°C), remove from the heat. Remove the sachet of lemon rinds with tongs, squeezing any excess liquid into the pot, and discard. This is a good time for a plate test.

Spoon a little of the jam onto a frozen saucer. Put the plate back in the freezer for 1 minute, then slide a finger through the jam. It's done when it parts and you see a strip of clean saucer. If it isn't set, return the pot to the heat, stir frequently, and test after another minute.

To Sqirl away your jam, see pages 16–21.

BLACKBERRY–MEYER LEMON JAM

Meyer lemons are a big part of what we do, and we preserve many of them year-round for our sorrel pesto bowl. The zest of Meyer lemons is pungent and has a floral aspect to its citrus scent. Nicely herbaceous, too. So it's great with juicy blackberries.

Makes 8 half-pint jars

INGREDIENTS

2,000 g (4 lb 6 oz)	**blackberries**
1,200 g (6 cups)	**sugar** (60% of the weight of blackberries)
40 g (2 Tbsp plus 2 tsp)	**lemon juice** (2% of the weight of blackberries)
1 Tbsp	**finely grated Meyer lemon zest**

Steven Murray of Murray Family Farms

Blackberry–Meyer lemon jam Berries

Prepare your plate test by putting a few saucers in the freezer.

If you have more or less than 2,000 g blackberries, you can figure out how much sugar and lemon juice you need by using the following formula:

Grams of blackberries × 0.60 = grams of sugar
Grams of blackberries × 0.02 = grams of lemon juice

Put the blackberries in a food processor and pulse until they are chopped but still a little chunky. (Alternatively, you can put the berries in a large bowl and crush them with your hands. Or for a mix of textures, puree half the berries in the food processor and squeeze the other half with your hands.)

Transfer the berries to a large bowl and stir in the sugar and lemon juice; let sit for at least a few minutes or up to 30 minutes, if you have the time. (You also have the option to use the plumping technique; see "Blending and Plumping" on page 14.)

Pour the mixture into your jamming pot.

Cook over high heat, stirring and scraping the bottom of the pot so the sugars don't burn. Use a spider or fine mesh skimmer to skim off any scum. (There won't be a lot, but there'll be some.) If the jam is bubbling more than you can manage, it's okay to turn off the heat, skim, then turn the heat back on. Dip the spider into a bowl of water and shake off any excess to clean between skims.

As the jam cooks, the solids will separate from the liquids and then rejoin. You'll see the surface will look matte at the beginning, then it will suddenly change to shiny and glossy. Sometimes with blackberry jam, the surface will form what look like dry patches. This indicates that the jam is nearly done. The temperature will reach 215°F (102°C) when done, about 28 minutes. When the jam nears this temperature, remove the pot from the heat and add the Meyer lemon zest. This is a good time for a plate test.

Spoon a little bit of jam onto a frozen saucer. Put the plate back in the freezer for 1 minute, then slide a finger through the jam. It's done when it parts and you see a strip of clean saucer. If it isn't set, return the pot to the heat, stir frequently, and test after another minute.

To Sqirl away your jam, see pages 16–21.

Variation:
Blackberry jam with lemon verbena

Skip the Meyer lemon zest and instead put about 5 g (¼ cup) fresh lemon verbena leaves in a cheesecloth sachet tied with kitchen string. Add it to the jamming pot along with the blackberries, sugar, and lemon juice. (Omit the Meyer lemon zest.) Remove the cheesecloth sachet when the temperature nears 215°F (102°C) and discard. Test as above.

BOYSENBERRY JAM

Boysenberry is a very California berry, a cross between a raspberry, blackberry, dewberry, and loganberry that can be traced to a grower named Boysen in Anaheim. Walter Knott, as in Knott's Berry Farm, was the first to grow them commercially in Southern California and named them boysenberries. (Knott's Berry boysenberry jam was what I grew up thinking of as jam.) Fresh boysenberries are especially juicy and are prone to break down within a few days, which means they aren't widely available. We used to get ours for Sqirl from Robert Poole, a retired math teacher who was one of the only remaining local growers. As of right now, we can only get them from Murray Family Farms. If you can find them, jam them!

Makes 8 half-pint jars

INGREDIENTS

2,000 g (4 lb 6 oz) **boysenberries**
1,100 g (5½ cups) **sugar** (55% of the weight of boysenberries)
60 g (¼ cup) **lemon juice** (3% of the weight of boysenberries)

Prepare your plate test by putting a few saucers in the freezer.

If you have more or less than 2,000 g boysenberries, you can figure out how much sugar and lemon juice you need by using the following formula:

Grams of blackberries × 0.55 = grams of sugar
Grams of blackberries × 0.03 = grams of lemon juice

Put the boysenberries in a food processor and pulse until they are chopped but still a little chunky. (Alternatively, you can put the berries in a large bowl and crush them with your hands. Or, for a mix of textures, puree half the berries in the food processor and squeeze the other half with your hands.)

Transfer the berries to a large bowl and stir in the sugar and lemon juice; let sit for at least a few minutes or up to 30 minutes if you have the time. (You also have the option to use the plumping technique here; see "Blending and Plumping" on page 14.)

Pour the mixture into your jamming pot.

Cook over high heat, stirring and scraping the bottom of the pot so the sugars don't burn. Use a spider or fine-mesh skimmer to skim off any scum. (There won't be a lot, but there'll be some.) If the jam is bubbling more than you can manage, it's okay to turn off the heat, skim, then turn the heat back on. Dip the spider into a bowl of water and shake off any excess to clean between skims.

As the jam cooks, the solids will separate from the liquids and then rejoin. You'll see the surface will look matte at the beginning, then it will suddenly change to shiny and glossy. The surface might form what look like dry patches. This indicates that the jam is nearly done. The temperature will reach 215°F (102°C) when done, about 25 minutes.

A few degrees before the jam reaches this temperature, spoon a little bit of jam onto a frozen saucer. Put the plate back in the freezer for 1 minute, then slide a finger through the jam. It's done when it parts and you see a strip of clean saucer. If it isn't set, return the pot to the heat, stir frequently, and test after another minute.

To Sqirl away your jam, see pages 16–21.

Boysenberry jam Berries

Boysenberry-apricot jam Berries

BOYSENBERRY-APRICOT JAM

Boysenberries and apricots make their appearance at the same time of year. So in late spring I have boysenberries. And I have apricots—these firm, thickly textured stone fruits that you want to soften a bit. The juices released by the boysenberries help smooth out the texture of the apricots. You can use boysenberries for their moisture, and their color, and some sweetness. Springtime simpatico.

Instead of boysenberries, you can use olallieberries, for olallieberry-apricot jam. Or apriums instead of apricots, for boysenberry-aprium. Or substitute both boysenberries and apricots with olallieberries and peaches, for olalliberry-peach jam. We've made all of these renditions with the 60% berries and 40% stone fruit, using the same amount of sugar and lemon juice.

Makes about 8 half-pint jars

INGREDIENTS

860 g (1 lb 14 oz)	**apricots** (800 g when pitted)
1,200 g (2 lb 10 oz)	**boysenberries**
1,100 g (5½ cups)	**sugar** (55% of the weight of pitted apricots plus boysenberries)
60 g (¼ cup)	**lemon juice** (3% of the weight of pitted apricots plus boysenberries)

Prepare your plate test by putting a few saucers in the freezer.

Cut the apricots in half and remove and discard the pits. Cut the apricot halves into quarters so that you have eight wedges per apricot. Put them in a large bowl and set aside.

You should have 800 g pitted apricots and 1,200 g boysenberries (40% apricots and 60% boysenberries). If you have more or less, you can figure out how much sugar and lemon juice you need by using the following formula:

Grams of pitted apricots plus boysenberries × 0.55 = grams of sugar
Grams of pitted apricots plus boysenberries × 0.03 = grams of lemon juice

Put the boysenberries in a food processor and pulse until they are chopped but still a little chunky. Combine the berries, sugar, and lemon juice with the apricots. (You have the option to use the plumping technique; see "Blending and Plumping" on page 14.) Transfer the mixture to your jamming pot.

Cook over high heat, stirring and scraping the bottom of the pot with a heatproof spatula so the sugars don't burn. Use a spider or fine-mesh skimmer to skim off any scum. If the jam is bubbling more than you can manage, it's okay to turn off the heat, skim, then turn the heat back on. Dip the spider into a large bowl of water and give it a shake to clean between skims.

After about 15 minutes, start smashing the fruit with a potato masher to break down the apricots.

As the jam cooks, the solids will separate from the liquid and then rejoin. You'll see the surface will look matte at the beginning, then it will suddenly change to shiny and glossy. Sometimes the surface will form what look like dry patches. The jam is done when it reaches about 215°F (102°C), about 28 minutes total. A few degrees before the jam reaches this temperature, perform a plate test.

Spoon a little bit of jam onto a frozen saucer. Put the plate back in the freezer for 1 minute, then slide a finger through the jam. It's done when it parts and you see a strip of clean saucer. If it isn't set, return the pot to the heat, stir frequently, and test after another minute.

To Sqirl away your jam, see pages 16–21.

THE TAYBERRY INCIDENT

Samin Nosrat, of Salt, Fat, Acid, Heat, posted Tayberries on her Instagram over the summer, and I knew I had to have them. So she helped me get in touch with a farmer in Santa Cruz County to secure some Tayberries—a cross between a raspberry and a blackberry (named after the river Tay in Scotland).

It was a little late in the season, but I flew up and was able to purchase four flats! I filled a Cambro container with fruit and taped it up with what I could find . . . fabric tape. Then I put the Cambro in my luggage and checked it in for a one-hour flight from San Jose to L.A. And that's where my troubles started.

I arrived at the airport in San Jose early (kind of smug about it), so I was sitting at my gate in the terminal waiting to board when I heard my name being called on the loudspeaker. I approached the woman at the gate's front desk, and she said, "You're in trouble. I heard your bag is a mess. You have to go back down to baggage check."

I started to feel panicky. Tim and Sue, two security guards from Southwest, were down there, and my bag was just leaking juice everywhere. Everywhere! It was so hot at the time that the berries had macerated themselves

in this Cambro. I had weirdly put my clothes in the side pouches, and they were miraculously untouched. But everything in the main compartment was soup.

Tim and Sue were stern: "You can't get on this flight. You're going to miss it. You've got to throw this away."

I was distraught and responded, "Oh my god. Each flat was a ridiculous amount of money. I just spent hundreds of dollars on these berries. This is a berry we can't get in LA. It's really special. Please help me. We have to save these Tayberries!"

I must have looked tragic. Because just like that, Tim and Sue turned it around. All of a sudden, they were like, "We have to save the berries! Here's an extra case we aren't using." Unbelievably, they had a random piece of luggage on hand, something semi-busted that someone had left behind.

They took the Cambro and wrapped it all up with extra tape. "Is it leaking? It's not leaking! Let's do this!" They swaddled it in two trash bags and put it in the suitcase.

I made it back to the gate, and all I could think was, "Oh my god, it's going to leak again." But Tim and Sue came and found me just to let me know it made it onto the flight. "Good luck with the Tayberries!"

And that is the story of the Tayberries of the summer of 2018. They went straight from the airport to Sqirl. I called Scott just so he could see them and juice was coming out everywhere again. We had to can them the same night—thirty-two jars of Tayberry jam that sold out immediately. Thanks, Tim and Sue.

TAYBERRY JAM

Tayberry, youngberry, marionberry, loganberry, and olallieberry—these are all special berries that we use for jam when we can find them. The best are soft, lush berries that practically disintegrate in your hands. Youngberries and loganberries I used to get from a grower in Redlands, but they are harder and harder to find. Marionberries I've only gotten from Oregon when visiting friends; they are to Oregon what boysenberries are to California: iconic and rare. Olallieberries from the town of Avila, California, are the juiciest, and these are in the regular Sqirl jam lineup. You can use this recipe for any of these berries, which are related to blackberries and raspberries.

Tayberry jam Berries

Makes about 8 half-pint jars

INGREDIENTS

2,000 g (4 lb 6 oz)   **Tayberries**
1,100 g (5½ cups)   **sugar** (55% of the weight of Tayberries)
80 g (¼ cup plus 1 Tbsp plus 1 tsp)   **lemon juice** (4% of the weight of Tayberries)

Prepare your plate test by putting a few saucers in the freezer.

If you have more or less than 2,000 g Tayberries, you can figure out how much sugar and lemon juice you need by using the following formula:

Grams of Tayberries × 0.55 = grams of sugar
Grams of Tayberries × 0.04 = grams of lemon juice

Put the berries in a food processor and pulse until they are chopped but still a little chunky. (Alternatively, you can put the berries in a large bowl and crush them with your hands. Or for a mix of textures, puree half the berries in the food processor and squeeze the other half with your hands.)

Transfer the berries to a large bowl and stir in the sugar and lemon juice; let sit for at least a few minutes or up to 30 minutes if you have the time. (You also have the option to use the plumping technique; see "Blending and Plumping" on page 14.)

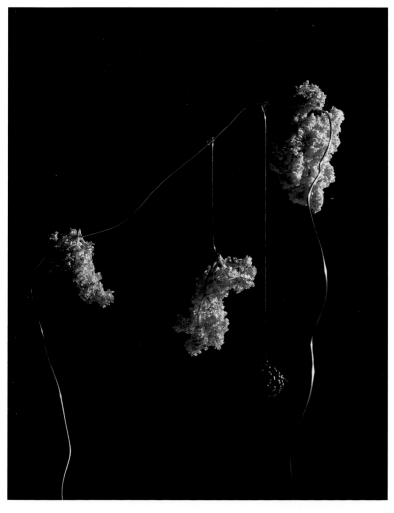

Pour the mixture into your jamming pot. Cook over high heat, stirring and scraping the bottom of the pot so the sugars don't burn. Use a spider or fine-mesh skimmer to skim off any scum. If the jam is bubbling more than you can manage, it's okay to turn off the heat, skim, then turn the heat back on. Dip the spider into a bowl of water and shake off any excess to clean between skims.

As the jam cooks, the solids will separate from the liquid and then rejoin. You'll see the surface become shiny and glossy, and sometimes it will form what look like dry, waxy patches. This indicates that the jam is nearly done. The temperature will reach about 217°F (103°C) when done, about 20 minutes. When the jam nears this temperature, perform a plate test.

Remove from the heat and spoon a little bit of jam onto a frozen saucer. Put the plate back in the freezer for 1 minute, then slide a finger through the jam. It's done when it parts and you see a strip of clean saucer. If it isn't set, return the pot to the heat, stir frequently, and test after another minute.

To Sqirl away your jam, see pages 16–21.

Variation:
Olallieberry jam with elderflower

Replace the Tayberries with olallieberries. Put 17 g (½ cup) fresh elderflowers in a cheesecloth sachet tied with kitchen string. (You have the option to use the plumping technique here; see "Blending and Plumping" on page 14.) Combine the olallieberries, sugar, lemon juice, and elderflower sachet in a pot and bring it to a boil. When it comes to a boil, remove from the heat. Transfer to a heatproof (such as Pyrex) container and let cool. Put the mixture in the refrigerator overnight to steep. The next day, cook the jam as above, removing and discarding the sachet when the jam is done.

There isn't a more loved jam in America than strawberry jam. It's actually one of the harder jams to make. I think people think, "Cute! Strawberry jam! How hard can it be to make?" Because of the water content it can be the most violent. Behind the angelic appearance is a secret demon. (We've all dated people like that.)

Classic strawberry jam Berries

Makes 8 half-pint jars

INGIREDIENTS

2,275 g (5 lbs)	**strawberries** (2,000 g trimmed)
1,200 g (6 cups)	**sugar** (60% of the weight of strawberries)
40 g (2 Tbsp plus 2 tsp)	**lemon juice** (2% of the weight of strawberries), plus the lemon rinds

Trim the tops off the strawberries and cut them in half lengthwise. You should have 2,000 g trimmed strawberries. If you have more or less, you can figure out how much sugar and lemon juice you need by using the following formula:

Grams of trimmed strawberries x 0.60 = grams of sugar
Grams of trimmed strawberries x 0.02 = grams of lemon juice

Put the berries in a food processor and pulse until pureed. (Alternatively, you can put the berries in a large bowl and crush them with your hands. Or for a mix of textures, puree half the berries in the food processor and squeeze the other half with your hands.) Pour the strawberries into a large bowl and stir in the sugar and lemon juice. (Don't throw out the lemon rinds.)

Let the fruit sit for at least 30 minutes. (You also have the option to use the plumping technique; see "Blending and Plumping" on page 14.) It's even better if you can let it sit overnight in the refrigerator, so the fruit will absorb more sugar and take less time to cook. It will also be less violent when it bubbles.

Transfer the strawberry mixture to your jamming pot. Put the lemon rinds in a cheesecloth sachet tied with kitchen string. Cook over high heat, continuously stirring and scraping the bottom of the pot so the sugars don't burn. Skim off any scum that forms on the surface of the jam. Turn off or lower the heat to avoid getting splattered with hot bubbles, use a spatula to round up all the scum, then remove it with a spider or fine-mesh strainer. Dip the spider into a bowl of water, shaking off the excess, to clean between skims. Turn the heat back on or up.

Keep in mind that the goal is to cook the jam in the shortest amount of time possible so that there's very little caramelization of the sugars. You won't be able to get all the scum. At some point, it just starts pulling back into the jam. Make sure you protect yourself with gloves.

Continue cooking and skimming until the jam is clear and the bubbles are smaller, 20 to 30 minutes. To check for doneness, it is tricky to get close enough to measure the temperature of this jam (because of all that violent bubbling). It should be about 216°F (102°C)—just remember that it's better to start testing for doneness sooner rather than later. When it nears this temperature, remove from the heat. Use tongs to lift up the bag and squeeze out all the liquid inside.

You really want to squeeze all the pectin from the lemon rinds into the pot because strawberries have only a small amount of natural pectin. Remove the bag and discard the rinds. This is a good time for a plate test.

Spoon a little of the jam onto a frozen saucer. Put the plate back in the freezer for 1 minute, then slide a finger through the jam. It's done when it parts and you see a strip of clean saucer. If it isn't set, return the pot to the heat, stir frequently, and test after another minute.

To Sqirl away your jam, see pages 16–21.

Variations:
Strawberry jam with honey

Replace half of the sugar with honey by weight.

Strawberry jam with jalapeño

Add 1 or 2 jalapeños, cut into pieces, to the lemon rinds in the cheesecloth sachet to get the heat without the seeds.

Strawberry jam with rose geranium

See pages 196–97 in *Everything I Want to Eat: Sqirl and the New California Cooking* for the recipe.

Mara des Bois—tiny French strawberries with maximum flavor—are spring and fall berries. They don't grow in the heat. "Oh, it's summer, and I want strawberries," you might think. That's not Mara des Bois. We get ours from Chino Farm in Rancho Santa Fe. They're the essence of strawberry. Floral, with incredible color and that uber-strawberry flavor. Because they're also delicate, they're cut from the stem—so they're nice to work with. Treat them in a very French style. (See "Blending and Plumping" on page 14.) You can make this in a single long day, or even just puree the berries in a food processor and cook them right away, but ideally you should let the strawberries macerate overnight twice: The first day, just cut the fruit and let the berries macerate. The second day, bring them to a boil, then let them sit overnight again. On the third day, bring them to a boil again until you have pure-joy strawberry jam.

Mara des Bois strawberry jam Berries

Makes 7 half-pint jars

INGREDIENTS

1,850 g (4 lb 1 oz)	**Mara des Bois strawberries** (1,650 g trimmed)
908 g (4½ cups)	**sugar** (55% of the weight of trimmed strawberries)
66 g (¼ cup plus 1 tsp)	**lemon juice** (4% of the weight of trimmed strawberries)

Tom Chino of Chino Farm holds the essence of strawberry.

Prepare your plate test by putting a few saucers in the freezer.

Trim the tops off the strawberries.

You should have about 1,650 g strawberries. If you have more or less, you can figure out how much sugar and lemon juice you need by using the following formula:

Grams of trimmed strawberries × 0.55 = grams of sugar
Grams of trimmed strawberries × 0.04 = grams of lemon juice

Put the strawberries in a large bowl and stir in the sugar and lemon juice. Cover the mixture with parchment paper directly touching the fruit and let sit for 3 to 4 hours, or overnight in the refrigerator.

Transfer the mixture to your jamming pot and bring it to a boil. Immediately remove from the heat and let cool. Transfer to a heatproof (such as Pyrex) container and let cool. Cover. Let the mixture rest again for 3 to 4 hours, or overnight in the refrigerator.

Put the mixture in your jamming pot and bring to a boil. Cook over high heat, continuously stirring and scraping the bottom of the pot so the sugars don't burn. Skim off any scum that forms on the surface of the jam. Turn off or lower the heat to avoid getting splattered with hot bubbles. Make sure you protect yourself with gloves. Use a spatula to round up all the scum, then remove it with a spider or fine-mesh strainer. Dip the spider into a bowl of water, shaking off the excess, to clean between skims. Turn the heat back on or up.

Keep in mind that the goal is to cook the jam in the shortest amount of time possible so that there's very little caramelization of the sugars. You won't be able to get all the scum. At some point, it just starts pulling back into the jam.

Continue cooking and skimming until the jam is clear and bubbling, about 20 minutes. It should be reduced by about half and the temperature will reach about 217°F (103°C). When it nears this temperature, perform a plate test.

Remove from the heat. Spoon a little of the jam onto a frozen saucer. Put the plate back in the freezer for 1 minute, then slide a finger through the jam. It's done when it parts and you see a strip of clean saucer. If it isn't set, return the pot to the heat, stir frequently, and test after another minute.

To Sqirl away your jam, see pages 16–21.

Variation:
Strawberry jam with red verjus

When the strawberry jam nears 217°F (103°C), remove from the heat and stir in 2 Tbsp red verjus until combined. This is a good time for your plate test.

FUMIO MAKES JAM (NSFH–NOT SAFE FOR HOME)

Let's talk about my friend Fumio. I'm actually a very technical jammer. Fumio? He's an artist who makes jam like no one else I've ever seen. (And by the way, don't try this at home.)

Fumio has a personal kitchen lab on his family's fifty-acre farm in Rancho Santa Fe. It's a no-shoes space, and he's usually inclined to remove not just his chanclas but also his socks. So he's standing barefoot, ladling hot-as-hell jam directly from a pot on the stove into a glass jar-that he's holding with his bare hands.

The jam? It's a syrup that he's taken to the hard crack stage (that's 300 to 310°F), to which he has added whole trimmed strawberries. He doesn't use lemon juice, he doesn't skim, he barely stirs-it's exactly the opposite of the way I make jam. But RESPECT. Because it has become his art, and he has developed his own techniques for making preserves, honed over years of experimentation.

Why doesn't he use lemon juice? To him, lemon juice messes with the full flavor of the fruit. (Lemon juice is widely accepted as an inherent part of jam making because, for one, it helps lower the pH so that the pectin released from the fruit can "set," and two, it helps balance the sweetness of the fruit.)

He uses only distilled water for processing because it doesn't have calcium. Calcium in, say, tap water can leave small white deposits on your jam lids. If this happens to you, know that it's harmless—just wipe your lids with a little white vinegar.

Other Fumio-isms include stacking the jam lids that he's going to use in a sort of interconnected circle in a water bath—lids placed on top of each other in a precise offset pattern—so that he can easily pick one up with tongs rather than the traditional magnet tool (a wand with a magnet on the very end so that the lid just sticks to the magnet and you can pick it up from hot water). And he adds water to his cranberry jam, something I'd never do, though his is lovely and soft. Note: Also, when he cans the jam he never heats up the jars prior to ladling jam in, and to my surprise they have never shattered. He also takes the two-piece lid, and once the ring is on, he turns it to the right until it's exceptionally tight. Then he flips the jars upside down—only flipping the jars right-side up when all the jam has been canned. My jaw was in a pcrmanently open position watching this. These are all things in contradiction to what I know. And . . . they work for him. Turns out there isn't just one way to make jam.

Also, all of his stone fruit is clingstone. It's what they have on the farm—most heritage varietals of stone fruit are clingstone. That means the flesh adheres to the pit—and it's hard to remove. (At Sqirl we find delicious freestone fruit so that removing the pit from the flesh is not excruciatingly tedious.)

Fumio Makes Jam

A tip from Fumio about peeling stone fruit such as peaches: You don't have to score it first. I score peaches, for example, with an X so that they're potentially easier to peel after they've been blanched. Fumio skips the scoring; he says water that seeps into the X crevice can dilute the flavor. There's no challenging Fumio; scoring isn't mandatory.

And his collection of jams? He has apricot and boysenberry jams that he has canned in stand-up plastic pouches. A pear conserve from 2014, in which the slices of pear are almost completely transparent—a confiture that honors the fruit. And the strawberry jam of the day, another confiture that's pure artistry—pieces of whole strawberry suspended in a sweet syrup.

This is not how Sqirl makes jam. But it's how Fumio the artiste makes it. And I love him for it. It's honest and it's beautiful and it's his way.

Fumio Makes Jam

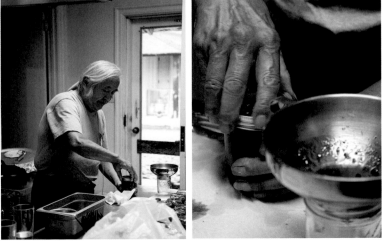

Top: A watched pot does boil . . . at some point.
Bottom: Fumio handles hot jam jars with his bare hands; you probably shouldn't.

Fumio Makes Jam

Pakistan mulberries are bizarrely long purple berries with musky raspberry overtones. They arrive at the markets long before Persian mulberries. I'm pretty sure they're the first berry of the season in Southern California, before blackberries even. It's easy to get excited about them—they're an indicator of what's to come. I'd never seen them as a jam before we started making it at the restaurant. They're fun to play with because of the way they look, and they're deeply flavored (but need more added acidity than other berries). This jam is great with a cheese plate.

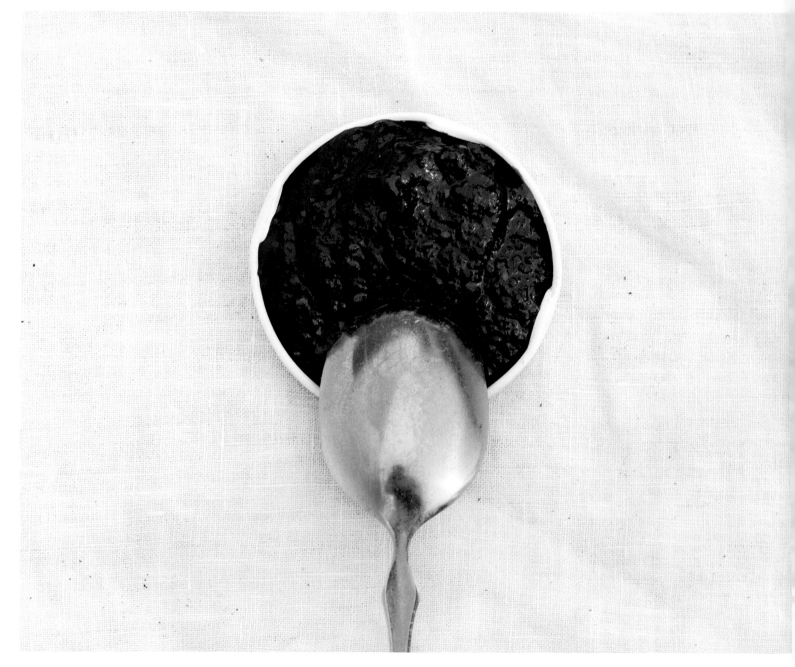

Pakistan mulberry jam Berries

Makes 8 half-pint jars

INGREDIENTS

2,000 g (4 lb 6 oz)   **Pakistan mulberries** (1,950 g destemmed)
1,072 g (5⅓ cups)   **sugar** (55% of the weight of destemmed mulberries)
60 g (¼ cup)   **lemon juice** (3% of the weight of destemmed mulberries)

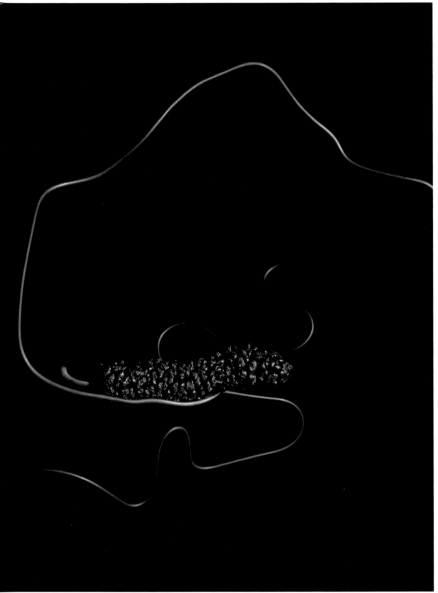

Prepare your plate test by putting a few saucers in the freezer.

Hold the stem of a mulberry and use your fingers to gently pull the fruit off the stem. Repeat with the remaining mulberries, getting as much fruit as possible, and discard the stems.

You should have 1,950 g destemmed mulberries. If you have more or less, you can figure out how much sugar and lemon juice you need by using the following formula:

Grams of destemmed mulberries × 0.55 = grams of sugar
Grams of destemmed mulberries × 0.03 = grams of lemon juice

Blend the mulberries in a food processor until pureed. (Alternatively, you can put the berries in a large bowl and crush them with your hands. Or for a mix of textures, puree half the berries in the food processor and squeeze the other half with your hands.) Pour the puree into a large bowl and mix in the sugar and lemon juice. You can jam this right away. Or for a silkier texture, let the berry mixture sit out for at least a few hours and up to overnight. (You also have the option to use the plumping technique here; see "Blending and Plumping" on page 14.)

Put the berry mixture in a jamming pot and cook over high heat, stirring and scraping the bottom of the pot with a heatproof spatula so the sugars don't caramelize too quickly and burn. Use a spider or fine-mesh skimmer to skim off any scum. Dip the spider into a bowl of water and shake off the excess to clean between skims.

It will have a lot of seeds, and it will look figgy and thick because of its seed-to-fruit ratio. You'll need to watch the temperature for doneness. When it nears 214°F (101°C), about 20 minutes, remove from the heat and perform a plate test.

Spoon a little bit of the jam onto a frozen saucer. Put the plate back in the freezer for 1 minute, then slide a finger through the jam. It's done when it parts and you see a strip of clean saucer. If it isn't set, return the pot to the heat, stir frequently, and test after another minute.

To Sqirl away your jam, see pages 16–21.

Persian mulberries: Oh my god, I love them. They're so delicate and beautiful. You pull the ripe fruit off the tree and your fingers are bloody with Persian mulberry juice. They don't live well once removed from the tree. You pick them and you have to use them right away. I'll start to get Facebook messages from Bettina Birch just before she harvests her mulberry bush—I think it's just the one bush, which she calls "Mother Mulberry." Once she harvests, she sends them every week in Igloos, which we have to return. It's a unique relationship, and my life is full of them. By the time the berries get to me, it's been a good twelve hours. There are ice packs in the cooler, but the berries are already seeping juice, which we use for agua fresca (just add water and honey to make a drink out of it).

Makes 8 half-pint jars

INGREDIENTS

2,300 g (5 lb 1 oz) **mulberries**
1,334 g (6⅔ cups) **sugar** (58% of the weight of mulberries)
46 g (3 Tbsp) **lemon juice** (2% of the weight of mulberries)

Prepare your plate test by putting a few saucers in the freezer.

If you have more or less than 2,300 g mulberries, you can figure out how much sugar and lemon juice you need by using the following formula:

Grams of mulberries × 0.58 = grams of sugar
Grams of mulberries × 0.02 = grams of lemon juice

Put the mulberries, sugar, and lemon juice in a large bowl and use your hands to mix, breaking up the berries as you combine. Let the mixture sit for at least a few hours and up to overnight in the refrigerator. (You also have the option to use the plumping technique here; see "Blending and Plumping" on page 14.)

Put the berry mixture in a jamming pot and cook over high heat, stirring and scraping the bottom of the pot with a heatproof spatula so the sugars don't caramelize too quickly and burn. Use a spider or fine-mesh skimmer to skim off any scum. Dip the spider into a bowl of water and shake off the excess to clean between skims.

As you stir and skim, check the temperature for doneness. When it nears 219°F (103°C), about 20 minutes, remove from the heat and perform a plate test.

Spoon a little bit of the jam onto a frozen saucer. Put the plate back in the freezer for 1 minute, then slide a finger through the jam. It's done when it parts and you see a strip of clean saucer. If it isn't set, return the pot to the heat, stir frequently, and test after another minute.

To Sqirl away your jam, see pages 16–21.

Brown rice porridge recipe in *Everything I Want to Eat*, p. 56

Persian mulberry jam Berries

BROWN BUTTER BLONDIES

These brown butter blondies are an iteration of a recipe from Max Lesser, who was running Morning Glory Confections. He and I were at the farmers' market selling our stuff, and these were so amazing that I asked him for the recipe and if we could translate it to Sqirl. Use raspberry jam, or any blue or red variety.

Brown butter blondies Berries

Makes 1 (8-inch/20 cm) square pan

INGREDIENTS

454 g (2 cups/4 sticks)	**unsalted butter**
522 g (2⅓ lightly packed cups)	**brown sugar**
2 tsp	**fine sea salt**
3	**large eggs**
1½ tsp	**vanilla extract**
384 g (3 cups plus 1 Tbsp)	**all-purpose flour**
1½ tsp	**baking powder**
	jam
75 g (¼ cup)	**Flaky sea salt**
	(such as Maldon) **to taste**

Heat the oven to 325°F (165°C).

Line an 8-inch (20 cm) square baking pan with parchment paper so that there's a 1-inch overhang and spray it with baking spray. Set aside.

Make brown butter: Put the butter in a saucepan over medium-high heat. When the butter starts foaming, start whisking. Cook the butter, continuing to whisk, until dark amber and nutty, 7 to 10 minutes, depending on the heat and the liquid content of your butter. Remove from the heat immediately.

You'll need 340 g (¾ cup) brown butter for this recipe. (Don't throw out any extra; just keep it in the refrigerator for another use.) While it's still warm, combine the brown butter with the brown sugar and salt in a mixing bowl and stir until incorporated. Stir the eggs and vanilla into the mixture until it becomes thick and glossy.

Using a rubber spatula, gently fold in the flour and baking powder and mix only until just incorporated. Pour the batter into the prepared pan. Spoon dollops of the jam on top of the batter and swirl the jam with a butter knife or skewer. Sprinkle with flaky sea salt as desired (I like it salty).

Bake until a tester inserted in the center comes out clean, 35 to 40 minutes. Let cool.

Remove the blondies from the pan in one piece by lifting the parchment. Transfer to a cutting board and cut it into 12 pieces. Store in an airtight container at room temperature for up to a few days (or in the freezer for a few months).

Brown butter blondies Berries

LINZER TORTE

I grew up eating tons of hamantaschen (jam-filled cookies—see recipe on page 124), and this is basically a big version of that.

Makes 1 (11-inch/28 cm) tart

INGREDIENTS

90 g (¾ cup)	**hazelnuts**
485 g (3⅔ cups plus 3 Tbsp)	**all-purpose flour**
150 g (¾ cup)	**sugar**
266 g (1 cup plus 3 Tbsp)	**unsalted butter, softened**
	Grated zest of 1 lemon
½ tsp	**fine sea salt**
2	**egg yolks**
375 g (1¼ cups)	**jam**
	Powdered sugar
	Whipped cream for serving

Put the hazelnuts and 85 g (⅔ cup) of the flour in a food processor and pulse until the mixture is the texture of coarsely ground cornmeal. Transfer the mixture to a large bowl and whisk in the remaining 400 g (3 cups plus 3 Tbsp) flour until well combined. Set aside.

In the bowl of a stand mixer fitted with a paddle attachment, combine the sugar, butter, lemon zest, and salt. Mix on medium speed until light and fluffy, 3 to 4 minutes. Add the egg yolks and mix until combined.

Working in three batches, add the flour-hazelnut mixture to the mixer; mix on low speed each time.

Divide the dough into two pieces, one slightly larger (about 550 g dough) than the other (about 440 g). Form the larger piece of dough into a disk and the smaller one into a rectangle about 1 inch (2.5 cm) thick and wrap in plastic. Let these rest in the refrigerator for 3 to 4 hours.

Heat the oven to 350°F (175°C). Grease and flour an 11-inch (28 cm) fluted tart pan. Remove the larger piece of dough from the fridge and place it between two pieces of floured parchment. Roll the dough into a 12-inch (30.5 cm) circle about ⅛ inch (3 mm) thick and transfer it to the tart pan. Gently pat the dough into the corners of the tart pan and trim the edges. Refrigerate or freeze until firm.

Roll out the smaller piece of dough into an 11-inch (28 cm) square. Cut the dough into ¾-inch (2 cm) strips and put these in the refrigerator to chill.

Spread the jam in the tart pan in an even layer. Remove the strips from the refrigerator. Form a lattice on top of the jam. With the remaining dough scraps, create a ½-inch (1.25 cm) border along the edge of the tart, gently pressing it into the edge of the tart pan. Score with the edge of a spoon or fork to create a pattern along the border.

If the dough is difficult to work with at any point in time, put it back in the refrigerator to chill for 5 to 10 minutes and try working with it again.

Bake until the crust is golden brown and the jam is bubbling, 35 to 45 minutes. Let cool. Dust with powdered sugar and serve with whipped cream. Wrap in plastic on a baking sheet and store at room temperature for up to two days.

Linzer torte Berries

RHUBARB

76–85

Rhubarb jam[76], Raspberry-rhubarb jam[78], Blueberry-rhubarb jam[80], Strawberry-rhubarb jam[82], Rhubarb-kumquat jam[84]

Rhubarb

Rhubarb is a miracle vegetable (that tastes like a fruit). The great thing about rhubarb is that it gives its whole self to your jam. It has to do with its relatively low water content. Strawberries have so much water that a lot of the fruit just evaporates while you're cooking. Rhubarb has less moisture content so you get more jam for your buck. Plus you know I love acidity, and it has it in spades.

Rhubarb jam Rhubarb

Makes about 9 half-pint jars

INGREDIENTS

2,000 g (4 lb 6 oz)	**trimmed rhubarb**
1,000 g (5 cups)	**sugar** (50% of the weight of trimmed rhubarb)
60 g (¼ cup)	**lemon juice** (3% of the weight of trimmed rhubarb)
	Grated zest of 1 orange (optional)

Prepare your plate test by putting a few saucers in the freezer.

Cut the rhubarb into ½-inch (1.25 cm) pieces; they should all be about the same size for even cooking.

If you have more or less than 2,000 g rhubarb, you can figure out how much sugar and lemon juice you need with the following formula:

Grams of rhubarb × 0.50 = grams of sugar
Grams of rhubarb × 0.03 = grams of lemon juice

Put the rhubarb, sugar, and lemon juice in a large pot and cook over high heat, stirring frequently, until their released liquid starts bubbling, about 14 minutes. Be careful that the bottom doesn't burn (stir once in a while). Reduce the heat to low and smash the rhubarb with a potato masher or wooden spoon until the rhubarb chunks are broken up, about 3 minutes. It won't be completely smooth but you don't want large pieces either.

Turn the heat back up to high and continue to cook, stirring frequently. Use a spider or fine-mesh skimmer to skim off any scum. Dip the spider into a bowl of water and shake off any excess to clean between skims.

Cook until the rhubarb jam is thickened and is a deep beautiful pink (overcooking might lead to loss of color) and the temperature reaches 214°F (101°C), about 21 minutes total. A few degrees before 214°F, remove from the heat. If using orange zest, add it now and stir until thoroughly mixed in. This is a good time for a plate test.

Spoon a little of the jam onto a frozen saucer. Put the plate back in the freezer for 1 minute, then slide a finger through the jam. It's done when it parts and you see a strip of clean saucer. If it isn't set, return the pot to the heat, stir frequently, and test after another 1 to 3 minutes.

To Sqirl away your jam, see pages 16–21.

Variation:
Rhubarb jam with lime zest

Replace lemon juice with lime juice and the zest of 1 orange with the zest of the limes you used for juicing.

Raspberries are expensive. Rhubarb isn't. So whenever you see an all-berry jam, now you know that it is relatively costly to make. (Hint-hint: That's why the Persian mulberry is $$$$$ a jar.)

Raspberry-rhubarb jam Rhubarb

Makes 8 half-pint jars

INGREDIENTS

800 g (1 lb 12 oz)	**rhubarb**
1,200 g (2 lb 10 oz)	**raspberries**
1,200 g (6 cups)	**sugar** (60% of the weight of raspberries plus rhubarb)
40 g (2 Tbsp plus 2 tsp)	**lemon juice** (2% of the weight of raspberries plus rhubarb)

Prepare your plate test by putting a few saucers in the freezer.

Cut the rhubarb into ¼-inch (6 mm) slices; they should all be about the same size for even cooking. Set aside.

Put the raspberries in a blender and puree until smooth.

If you have more or less than 2,000 g rhubarb and raspberries (we use 40% rhubarb and 60% raspberries), you can figure out how much sugar and lemon juice you will need by using the following formula:

Grams of rhubarb plus raspberries × 0.60 = grams of sugar
Grams of rhubarb plus raspberries × 0.02 = grams of lemon juice

Combine the raspberry puree, rhubarb, sugar, and lemon juice in a jamming pot. Cook over high heat, stirring frequently, for 15 minutes.

Reduce the heat to low. Smash the rhubarb with a potato masher or wooden spoon for 1 minute just to start breaking it down so that it eventually melts into the raspberry puree. (It won't fully break down—it's okay to have some chunks.) Turn the heat back up and cook for 5 minutes. Use a spider or fine-mesh skimmer to skim off any scum. Dip the spider into a bowl of water and shake off any excess to clean between skims.

Reduce the heat to low, and smash the rhubarb again for a minute or two. Turn the heat back up to high and cook (stirring and skimming when necessary) until the jam is thickened, the texture is homogenous, and the temperature reaches 213°F (101°C), about 22 minutes total. A few degrees before the jam reaches this temperature, remove from the heat and perform a plate test.

Spoon a little of the jam onto a frozen saucer. Put the plate back in the freezer for 1 minute, then slide a finger through the jam. It's done when it parts and you see a strip of clean saucer. If it isn't set, return the pot to the heat, stir constantly, and test again after 1 to 2 minutes.

To Sqirl away your jam, see pages 16–21.

Blueberry-rhubarb is the first berry jam that we made at Sqirl after marmalade season, a riff on a Southern classic. An iconic jam for me because it's what Sqirl's all about—taking a classic and turning it on its head.

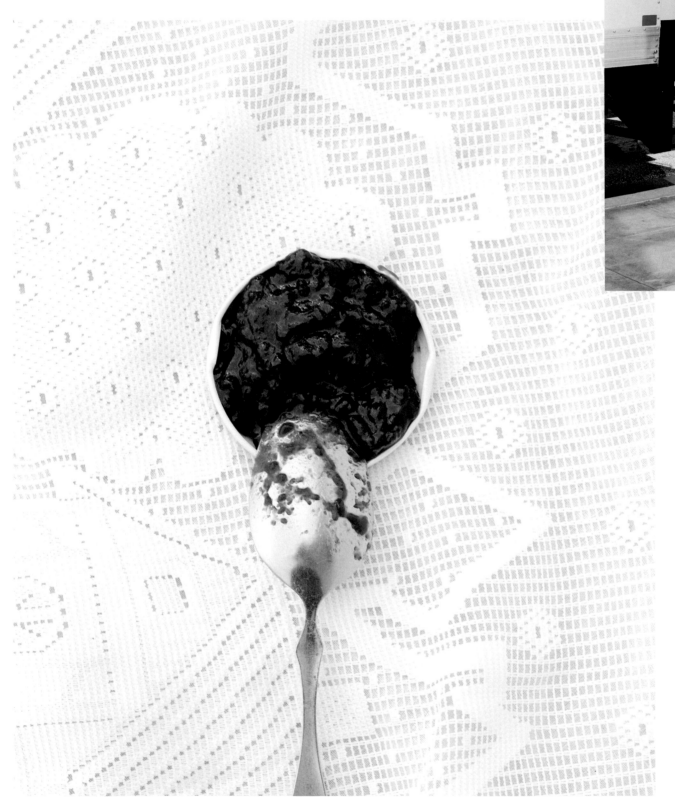

Blueberry-rhubarb jam Rhubarb

Makes 10 half-pint jars

INGREDIENTS

1,000 g (2 lb 3 oz)	**rhubarb**
1,000 g (2 lb 3 oz)	**blueberries**
1,200 g (6 cups)	**sugar** (60% of the weight of blueberries plus rhubarb)
40 g (2 Tbsp plus 2 tsp)	**lemon juice** (2% of the weight of blueberries plus rhubarb)

Prepare your plate test by putting a few saucers in the freezer.

Cut the rhubarb into ¼-inch (6 mm) slices; they should all be about the same size for even cooking. Set aside.

Put the blueberries in a blender and puree until smooth: Start with a little bit of the blueberries and blend on low speed as you add the rest of the berries and increase the speed.

If you have more or less than 2,000 g rhubarb and blueberries (we use 50% rhubarb and 50% blueberries), you can figure out how much sugar and lemon juice you will need by using the following formula:

Grams of rhubarb plus blueberries × 0.60 = grams of sugar
Grams of rhubarb plus blueberries × 0.02 = grams of lemon juice

Combine the blueberry puree, rhubarb, sugar, and lemon juice in a jamming pot. Cook the mixture over high heat, stirring frequently. When the rhubarb is softened, about 14 minutes, reduce the heat to low. Use a potato masher or wooden spoon to smash it; you're going to be stirring a lot because the fruit needs to disintegrate, release liquid, and eventually melt into the blueberry puree. (It won't fully break down—it's okay to have some chunks.)

Turn the heat back up to high and cook for 4 minutes, stirring. Use a spider or fine-mesh skimmer to skim off any scum. Dip the spider into a bowl of water and shake off any excess to clean between skims.

Reduce the heat to low, then smash the rhubarb again with a potato masher for a minute. Turn the heat back up to high and continue to cook, stirring and skimming as necessary, for another couple of minutes, until the jam is thickened, the texture is homogenous, and the temperature reaches 213°F (101°C), about 25 minutes total. Perform a plate test.

Spoon a little of the jam onto a frozen saucer. Put the plate back in the freezer for 1 minute, then slide a finger through the jam. It's done when it parts and you see a strip of clean saucer. If it isn't set, return the pot to the heat, stir constantly, and test again after 1 to 2 minutes.

To Sqirl away your jam, see pages 16–21.

And here's to making a classic the best it can be.

Strawberry-rhubarb jam Rhubarb

Makes 8 half-pint jars

INGREDIENTS

800 g (1 lb 12 oz)	**rhubarb**
1,370 g (3 lb)	**strawberries** (1,200 g trimmed)
1,200 g (6 cups)	**sugar** (60% of the weight of trimmed strawberries plus rhubarb)
40 g (2 Tbsp plus 2 tsp)	**lemon juice** (2% of the weight of trimmed strawberries plus rhubarb)

Prepare your plate test by putting a few saucers in the freezer.

Cut the rhubarb into ¼-inch (6 mm) slices; they should all be about the same size for even cooking. Set aside.

Trim the strawberries (you should have 1,200 g trimmed berries). If you have more or less than 2,000 g rhubarb and strawberries (we use 40% rhubarb and 60% blueberries), you can figure out how much sugar and lemon juice you will need by using the following formula:

Grams of rhubarb plus trimmed strawberries × 0.60 = grams of sugar
Grams of rhubarb plus trimmed strawberries × 0.02 = grams of lemon juice

Put the strawberries and lemon juice in a blender and puree until smooth. Combine the strawberry puree, sliced rhubarb, and sugar in a jamming pot. Cook over high heat, stirring frequently, until boiling, about 15 minutes.

Reduce the heat to low. Smash the rhubarb with a potato masher or wooden spoon for 1 minute. You want to start breaking it down so that it eventually melts into the strawberry puree. (It won't fully break down—it's okay to have some chunks.)

Turn the heat back up to high and cook for 5 minutes, stirring. Use a spider or fine-mesh skimmer to skim off any scum. Dip the spider into a bowl of water and shake off any excess to clean between skims.

Reduce the heat to low, then smash the rhubarb again with a potato masher or wooden spoon. Turn the heat back up to high and continue to cook, stirring and skimming as necessary, for another couple of minutes, until the jam is thickened, the texture is homogenous, and the temperature reaches 212°F (101°C), about 25 minutes total. A few degrees before the jam reaches this temperature, remove from the heat and perform a plate test.

Spoon a little of the jam onto a frozen saucer. Put the plate back in the freezer for 1 minute, then slide a finger through the jam. It's done when it parts and you see a strip of clean saucer. If it isn't set, return the pot to the heat, stir constantly, and test again after 1 to 2 minutes.

To Sqirl away your jam, see pages 16–21.

During the winter season there aren't a lot of things popping up here in Southern California other than citrus and rhubarb. So I had the idea to combine rhubarb and kumquats in a jam. My first attempt was a big fail. It turned out bitter because I used a lot more kumquats than rhubarb. So I thought, why don't I invert it? Now I love this jam, especially on ice cream.

When we have an overabundance of kumquats we'll puree and freeze them for future use. Cut the kumquats, remove the seeds, puree them in a high-speed blender; transfer the puree to a sealed container, and put it in the freezer for up to a year. The puree keeps really well and doesn't lose its flavor or texture.

Makes 8 half-pint jars

INGREDIENTS

1,500 g (3 lb 5 oz)	**rhubarb**
300 g (11 oz)	**kumquats**
1,065 g (5 cups plus scant ⅓ cup)	**sugar** (60% of the weight of rhubarb plus kumquat puree)
37 g (2 Tbsp plus 1 tsp)	**lemon juice** (2% of the weight of rhubarb plus kumquat puree)

Prepare your plate test by putting a few saucers in the freezer.

Cut the rhubarb into ¼-inch (6 mm) slices; they should all be about the same size for even cooking. Set aside.

Cut the kumquats in half crosswise, squeeze the halves for their juice into a bowl with a strainer and discard the seeds. Put the juice and the rinds in a blender and puree until smooth. You should have 270 g kumquat puree.

If you have more or less than 1,770 g rhubarb and kumquat puree (we use about 85% rhubarb and 15% kumquat puree), you can figure out how much sugar and lemon juice you will need by using the following formula:

Grams of rhubarb plus kumquat puree × 0.60 = grams of sugar
Grams of rhubarb plus kumquat puree × 0.02 = grams of lemon juice

Combine the rhubarb, kumquat puree, sugar, and lemon juice in your jamming pot. Cook over high heat, stirring frequently, for about 15 minutes. Reduce the heat to low. Smash the rhubarb with a potato masher or wooden spoon for 1 minute just to start breaking it down so that it eventually melts into kumquat puree. (It won't fully break down—it's okay to have some chunks.)

Turn the heat back up to high and continue to cook, stirring frequently. Use a spider or fine-mesh skimmer to skim off any scum. Dip the spider into a bowl of water and shake off any excess to clean between skims.

Cook until the jam is thickened, the texture is homogenous, and the temperature reaches 213°F (101°C), about 20 minutes total. A few degrees before the jam reaches this temperature, remove from the heat and perform a plate test.

Spoon a little of the jam onto a frozen saucer. Put the plate back in the freezer for 1 minute, then slide a finger through the jam. It's done when it parts and you see a strip of clean saucer. If it isn't set, return the pot to the heat, stir constantly, and test again after 1 to 2 minutes.

To Sqirl away your jam, see pages 16–21.

Rhubarb-kumquat jam Rhubarb

Stone Fruit
88-125

David Karp's Top 12[88], Strawberry-cherry jam[90], Strawberry-peach jam[92], Cherry jam[94], Sour cherry jam[96], Blenheim apricot jam[98], Snow Queen nectarine jam[100], June and Rich Lady peach jam[104], Variation: Elberta peach jam with lemon verbena[105], Variation: Silver Logan peach jam with sumac[105], Elephant Heart plum jam[106], Santa Rosa plum jam with flowering thyme[108], Mirabelle plum jam[112], Damson plum cheese[114], Plum chutney[116] Reine Claude jam[120], Honey Punch pluot jam[122], Hamantaschen[124]

Stone Fruit

DAVID KARP'S TOP 12

When I started Sqirl, David Karp—a pomologist also known as the Fruit Detective—was writing a weekly farmers' market report for the Los Angeles Times, and it was my bible. Because of him I discovered Walker Apples and Blenheim apricots. He brought certain farms to life.

Most people see a peach, and it's a peach. Not one of the dozens of varieties of peaches that are available at farmers' markets. It's overwhelming, even to a chef. David helped me navigate that world.

A few years ago he partnered with Andy Mariani of Andy's Orchard in Morgan Hill, California, bringing cherries, apricots, nectarines, plums, and peaches to the Santa Monica Farmers Market every week starting in June until the last of the peaches run out. He sends out a weekly newsletter describing each fruit in loving detail.

Here are David's Top 12 stone fruits for jamming and preserving. →

David Karp's Top 12

Santa Monica Farmers Market, Santa Monica, California

1 **Baby Crawford yellow peach** is arguably the finest of its kind, both for making preserves and for eating fresh. It has beautiful bright yellow skin, with just a hint of blush on a few fruits; gorgeous yellow flesh, with no red near the small free stone; and rich, spicy flavor, like a clingstone in a freestone peach. Bred at the University of California, Davis, it was an experimental selection rescued because it tasted like Yellow St. John, an elite Crawford-class peach once grown in California's Santa Clara Valley.

2 **Black Republican cherry** is a parent of the Bing, slightly later in harvest timing, and smaller in size, but with an even more intense flavor. It needs to be dead-ripe to be at its best, at which point it has a winy, dark, almost chocolaty flavor, with a distinctive "gout du noyau" (flavor of the nut). It's great to eat fresh, worthy of showcasing as a fine dessert by itself, and the classic cherry for making cherry ice cream, and it makes a uniquely dark, intense sweet cherry jam. A seedling of Black Eagle (or possibly a cross of Napoleon and Black Tartarian, by another account), it originated in the mid-nineteenth century in the Oregon orchard of Seth Lewelling, a Union sympathizer, who named the variety to annoy Confederate partisans.

3 **Blenheim apricot** was for more than a century the leading variety grown in California, mostly for drying and for preserves, and remains a home garden and farmers' market favorite. Ranging in size from small to medium, it can be pale yellow-orange, or deeper orange with a freckled, rosy blush; it has tender, juicy, luscious flesh and is honey-sweet, balanced by a tinge of acidity in specimens that are not overripe. Most vitally, Blenheim has a sensual perfume, a mysterious complexity lacking in most modern varieties. Too delicate to withstand the brutal heat of the San Joaquin Valley, it reaches perfection only when grown in intermediate coastal valleys.

4 **Bonny Royal apricot** is larger, firmer, higher in acidity, and juicier than Blenheim; it may be heresy, but many people say the flavor is more intense, and it arguably makes an even better jam. The fruit is a deep orange in color, juicy and very rich. It has tough skin and typically develops cracks at the stem end. Bonny Royal likely has Blenheim in its parentage and was first evaluated by George Bonacich, an apricot grower in Patterson, California.

5 **Damson plum** has dark blue, astringent skin and dry, sour flesh, so it's not good for eating fresh, but its tartness and spiciness are ideal for making preserves. Cooked down, the damson's astringency disappears, and its tannic skin imparts a gorgeous magenta color and rich, spicy flavor, while its abundant pectin confers a lusciously thick and smooth consistency. Originating in western Asia (supposedly near Damascus, whence its name), the damson is considered by scientists to be an ancestor of the sweeter and larger European plums.

6 **Elephant Heart plum** is large and heart-shaped; the skin is thick, mottled purple, brown, and green with heavy bloom. It is freestone, and the flesh is blood red and juicy, with a rich, distinctive flavor; it may require ripening after harvest. Elephant Heart is a favorite among fanciers of heirloom fruits. Perfect specimens are deep, deep purple, luscious, sweet, and intense. Its pedigree is unknown, but Satsuma appears likely to have been a parent or ancestor; it was selected by Luther Burbank in around 1920 and introduced in 1929 by Stark Bro's Nurseries.

7 **Flavor King Pluot** is one of the first and arguably the best of Floyd Zaiger's Pluots (plum-apricot interspecific crosses, with plum genes and characteristics predominant). The fruit is large, with dark reddish purple skin, red flesh, and incredibly rich and complex plum flavor, with hints of apricot and tropical fruit.

8 **Greengage European plum** is small, green, and unprepossessing in appearance, but when well grown and fully ripe the greengage has a pleasantly firm but juicy texture and is outrageously high in sugar, with good acidity, and a very strong, distinctive flavor. Of the same species (Prunus domestica) as the prune plums used for drying, it is far superior for eating fresh and making jam. It originated in the Caucasus and passed to us through Italy and then France, where it is known as Reine-Claude. A century ago, greengages were grown in northern California for canning and preserves, but they were supplanted by larger, showier, more productive Asian plums. Only a few farms in the United States have plantings today, but if Michelin rated fruits, greengages surely would merit three stars: "Worth a special journey."

9 **Raspberry Red nectarine** is small but highly flavored, with speckled burgundy skin, red and white flesh, abundant juice, and a luscious, complex flavor with sweetness, tartness, and lots of depth. This unique little variety was bred by Andy Mariani and the Santa Clara stone fruit breeding group in the Santa Clara Valley chapter of California Rare Fruit Growers.

10 **Santa Rosa Asian plum** was introduced by George C. Roeding of the Fancher Creek Nurseries, in Fresno, California, in 1906 or 1907. The fruit was large for its era (although it seems on the small side today) and roundish; the skin has purplish red skin with conspicuous dots and whitish bloom; it is clingstone. The flesh is yellow to dark red near the skin, rich, juicy, and aromatic, and delicious; it is tart near the skin and pit. It was described by its renowned breeder, Luther Burbank, as a complex hybrid of Asian plum, apricot plum, and a native North American plum, with the Asian plum predominating. Because of the variety's red flesh, he supposed that Satsuma was a parent or ancestor. Modern molecular studies have found that Santa Rosa did not have native American plum in its parentage, but it did have Prunus cerasifera (cherry plum).

11 **Silk Road yellow nectarines** are three very similar varieties (all sold as Silk Road) that are small and bright yellow-orange, with the intense tang and pleasant smack of astringency of a wild fruit, much like the original nectarines that grow wild in central Asia, where nectarines originated. Derived from seeds brought back by Andy Mariani from a fruit exploring trip in 1991, it's pure gold, fully freestone, with complex, intense flavor (but highly susceptible to postharvest rot).

12 **Snow Queen white nectarine**, the apotheosis of high flavor in stone fruit, ripens in June in California's San Joaquin Valley (stone fruit central). Bred by Armstrong Nurseries from unknown parents in the 1950s, it has speckled, leathery skin; dense, buttery, creamy white flesh that is preternaturally high in sweetness and acidity; and an intensely vinous nectarine aroma. The flesh of a top specimen is speckled with dots and swirls of red like some kind of edible, melting marble; when you bite in, there's a pleasant snap, and then the juice explodes in your mouth, revealing layer on layer of complex, interesting, super-pleasurable flavors and aromas, which linger and linger on the palate.

STRAWBERRY-CHERRY JAM

The epitome of summer is strawberries and cherries. (And watermelon. But watermelon doesn't make a great jam.)

Strawberry-cherry jam Stone Fruit

Makes 8 half-pint jars

INGREDIENTS

1,200 g (2 lb 10 oz)   **cherries**
1,500 g (3 lb 5 oz)   **trimmed, halved strawberries**
1,625 g (8 cups plus 2 Tbsp)   **sugar** (65% of the weight of trimmed strawberries plus pitted cherries)
125 g (½ cup plus 1 tsp)   **lemon juice** (5% of the weight of trimmed strawberries plus pitted cherries)

Prepare your plate test by putting a few saucers in the freezer.

Remove and discard the cherry stems. Use a pitter to remove the pits, and discard. You should have 1,000 g pitted cherries.

If you have more or less than 1,000 g cherries and 1,500 g strawberries (40% cherries and 60% strawberries), you can figure out how much sugar and lemon juice you need by using the following formula:

$$\text{Grams of pitted cherries plus trimmed strawberries} \times 0.65 = \text{grams of sugar}$$
$$\text{Grams of pitted cherries plus trimmed strawberries} \times 0.05 = \text{grams of lemon juice}$$

Puree the strawberries and cherries in a blender or food processor until as smooth as possible. Pour the pureed strawberry-cherry mixture into a large bowl and stir in the sugar and lemon juice. Let the fruit macerate for 30 minutes. (You also have the option to use the plumping technique; see "Blending and Plumping" on page 14.)

Transfer the mixture to your jamming pot and cook over high heat, continuously stirring and scraping the bottom of the pot so the sugars don't burn. Using a spider or fine-mesh skimmer, skim any scum that rises to the top. Dip the spider into a bowl of water and shake off the excess between skims to keep it clean.

Continue to stir and skim until the jam is thickened and reduced by about one-third. You also might notice waxy patches on the surface of the mixture. It's done when it reaches 217°F (103°C), about 32 minutes. When the jam nears this temperature, remove from the heat and perform a plate test.

Spoon a little of the jam onto a frozen saucer. Put the plate back in the freezer for 1 minute, then slide a finger through the jam. It's done when it parts and you see a strip of clean plate. If it isn't set, return the pot to the heat, stir constantly, and test again after 1 or 2 minutes.

To Sqirl away your jam, see pages 16–21.

STRAWBERRY-PEACH JAM

Strawberries and peaches—also the epitome of summertime. Let's call it the Epitome of Summer: Part Two.

Just remember: Stone fruit such as peaches, nectarines, plums, and apricots for jam should be ripe. The fruit shouldn't be crunchy at all, but it shouldn't be turning brown either.

Makes 8 half-pint jars

INGREDIENTS

½ Tbsp	**salt**
1,000 g (2 lb 3 oz)	**ripe peaches**
1,200 g (2 lb 14 oz)	**trimmed strawberries**
1,200 g (6 cups)	**sugar** (60% of the weight of trimmed strawberries plus pitted peaches)
40 g (2 Tbsp plus 2 tsp)	**lemon juice** (2% of the weight of trimmed strawberries plus pitted peaches)

We don't typically use donut peaches at Sqirl when canning, but Scott loves these. And if all you have are donut peaches, then use them!

Strawberry-peach jam Stone Fruit

Prepare your plate test by putting a few saucers in the freezer.

Bring a pot of water with the salt to a boil. Prepare an ice bath by filling a large bowl with ice and set aside.

Score the peaches with a sharp knife: Start at the pointed end of the peach and score an X that goes all the way around the circumference of the peach, being careful not to cut too deeply into the flesh.

Boil the peaches for 30 seconds and use a skimmer to transfer the peaches to the ice bath. When cool enough to handle, remove the skins, using your fingers. Cut the peaches in half. Remove the pits, making sure the halves are totally cleaned of all parts of the seed. You should have 800 g peaches.

If you have more or less than 800 g peaches and 1,200 g strawberries, you can figure out how much sugar and lemon juice you need with the following formula:

Grams of pitted peaches plus trimmed strawberries × 0.60 = grams of sugar
Grams of pitted peaches plus trimmed strawberries × 0.02 = grams of lemon juice

Put the peaches in a large bowl or container and smash them really well with your hands.

Puree the strawberries in a blender until smooth. Combine them with the peaches.

Mix the fruit with the sugar and lemon juice. (You have the option to use the plumping technique here; see "Blending and Plumping" on page 14.) Transfer the mixture to your jamming pot and cook over high heat, stirring and scraping the bottom of the pot so the sugars don't burn. Once it starts to boil, start smashing the fruit frequently with a potato masher. It will be somewhat chunky, but the pieces shouldn't be too big. Using a spider or fine-mesh skimmer, skim any scum that rises to the top. Avoid removing small pieces of peach. Dip the spider into a bowl of water and shake off the excess between skims to keep it clean. Cook the jam until thickened and the temperature reaches 211°F (99°C), about 23 minutes. When the jam nears this temperature, remove from the heat and perform a plate test.

Spoon a little of the jam onto a frozen saucer. Put the plate back in the freezer for 1 minute, then slide a finger through the jam. It's done when it parts and you see a strip of clean plate. If it isn't set, return the pot to the heat, stir constantly, and test again after 1 or 2 minutes.

To Sqirl away your jam, see pages 16–21.

Cherry jam is one of the ones I never thought I'd be able to make well. First, cherries take a ton of time because you have to pit them. Watch a good rom-com while you pit! Then on top of that there isn't a lot of pectin in cherries. So cherries are usually used for preserves—a loose, suspended-fruit-in-gel situation—rather than the smoother jams we tend to make at Sqirl. So what I'm going to tell you might not be what some traditionalists would do. But this has worked really well for me. I blend the cherries into a puree—I love the texture and it also helps draw out the pectin.

Cherry Jam Stone Fruit

Makes 10 half-pint jars

INGIREDIENTS

2,870 g (6 lb 5 oz)   **cherries**
126 g (½ cup plus 1 tsp)   **lemon juice** (5% of the weight of pitted cherries)
1,641 g (8 cups plus 2½ Tbsp) **sugar** (63% of the weight of pitted cherries)

Prepare your plate test by putting a few saucers in the freezer.

Remove and discard the cherry stems. Use a pitter to remove the pits, and discard. (Watch out for those double-seeded cherries. It's hard to remove cherry seeds from a pot of boiling jam.) You should have 2,525 g of pitted cherries.

If you have more or less cherries, you can figure out the amount of sugar and lemon juice you need by using the following formula:

Grams of pitted cherries × 0.63 = grams of sugar
Grams of pitted cherries × 0.05 = grams of lemon juice

Put the cherries and lemon juice in a blender and puree until it's as smooth as you can possibly get it (it's not going to be really fine). Blend a little at a time, starting on low and increasing the speed gradually. If you need to blend in batches, leave a little of the previous puree in the blender to help get the next batch going. (You have the option to use the plumping technique here; see "Blending and Plumping" on page 14.)

Combine the cherry puree and sugar in your jamming pot and cook over high heat, stirring and scraping the bottom of the pot so the sugars don't burn. There will be lots of skimming. Using a spider or fine-mesh skimmer, skim the scum that rises to the top. Dip the spider into a bowl of water and shake off the excess between skims to keep it clean. Cook the jam until the temperature reaches 218°F (103°C), about 22 minutes. The jam will be thicker, the bubbles smaller, and you might see waxy patches form on the surface. When the jam nears this temperature, remove from the heat and perform a plate test.

Spoon a little of the jam onto a frozen saucer. Put the plate back in the freezer for 1 minute, then slide a finger through the jam. It's done when it parts and you see a strip of clean plate. If it isn't set, return the pot to the heat, stir constantly, and test again after 1 or 2 minutes.

To Sqirl away your jam, see pages 16–21.

SOUR CHERRY JAM

California grows a lot of cherries, which usually show up in late April or early May, a true sign of spring. Sour cherries arrive later, and their season is short. There's a small window of time in which to catch these, so that's all the more reason to preserve them.

Makes about 5 half-pint jars

INGREDIENTS

2,150 g (4¾ lb)	**sour cherries**
93 g (2 Tbsp)	**lemon juice** (5% of the weight of pitted cherries)
1,214 g (6 cups plus 1 Tbsp)	**sugar** (65% of the weight of pitted cherries)

Prepare your plate test by putting a few saucers in the freezer.

Remove and discard the stems and pits of the cherries. You should have 1,868 g pitted cherries.

If you have more or less cherries, you can figure out the amount of sugar and lemon juice you need by using the following formula:

Grams of pitted cherries × 0.65 = grams of sugar
Grams of pitted cherries × 0.05 = grams of lemon juice

Put the cherries and lemon juice in a blender and puree until it's as smooth as you can possibly get it (it's not going to be really fine). Blend a little at a time, starting on low and increasing the speed gradually. If you need to blend in batches, leave a little of the previous puree in the blender to help get the next batch going. (You have the option to use the plumping technique here; see "Blending and Plumping" on page 14.)

Combine the cherry puree and sugar in your jamming pot and cook over high heat, stirring and scraping the bottom of the pot so the sugars don't burn. There will be lots of skimming. Using a spider or fine-mesh skimmer, skim the scum that rises to the top. Dip the spider into a bowl of water and shake off the excess between skims to keep it clean. After 10 minutes (or if it's boiling too vigorously to skim), reduce the heat to medium. Keep skimming and continue to cook; reduce the heat to medium-low as necessary to prevent the jam from bubbling over.

Cook until the temperature reaches 221°F (105°C), about 35 minutes. The jam will be thicker, the bubbles smaller, and you might see waxy patches form on the surface. (But it won't be a super thick jam; it'll look a lot like strawberry jam.)

When the jam nears this temperature, remove from the heat and perform a plate test. Spoon a little of the jam onto a frozen saucer. Put the plate back in the freezer for 1 minute, then slide a finger through the jam. It's done when it parts and you see a strip of clean plate. If it isn't set, return the pot to the heat, stir constantly, and test again after 1 or 2 minutes.

To Sqirl away your jam, see pages 16–21.

Sour cherries from Murray's, hanging out as we wait for our order at Zankou's Chicken in Hollywood.

BLENHEIM APRICOT JAM

Mild, honey-flavored Blenheim apricots hold a special place in the Sqirl canon of jams. Grown in California in the early 1900s, they later fell out of favor—too delicate to market widely. Now they're increasingly available at West Coast farmers' markets. They're beautifully balanced —tart and sweet—just what I look for in a fruit. But we do make a lot of adjustments to apricot jam from season to season. The amount of sugar might be as much as 60% of the fruit one season, while it might be 50% the next two seasons. Sometimes 2% lemon juice, sometimes 3% lemon juice. The key is to make a test batch and adjust.

Blenheim apricot jam Stone Fruit

Makes 7 half-pint jars

INGREDIENTS

2,046 g (4 lb 8 oz)	**whole apricots**
1,055 g (5¼ cups)	**sugar** (55% of the weight of pitted apricots)
38 g (2½ Tbsp)	**lemon juice** (2% of the weight of pitted apricots)

Apricots and apriums are usually freestone. That means the pit is easily separated from the fruit when it's ripe. Cut the fruit in half around the pit, pull out the seed, then cut each apricot half into three equal pieces. So each apricot is cut into 6 wedges (I know this sounds crazy, but the smaller pieces will be easier to smash as they cook). You should have 1,910 g pitted apricots.

If you have more or less apricots, you can figure out the amount of sugar and lemon juice you need by using the following formula:

Grams of pitted apricots × 0.55 = grams of sugar
Grams of pitted apricots × 0.02 = grams of lemon juice

(You have the option to use the plumping technique here; see "Blending and Plumping" on page 14.)

Combine the apricots with the sugar and lemon juice in your jamming pot and cook over high heat, stirring and scraping the bottom of the pot frequently. Once the apricots begin to soften, smash them with a potato masher as they cook. You can stir and smash at the same time. As the apricots cook the liquid will boil off, and that's when the jam will bubble up a lot. Be careful! Using a spider or fine-mesh skimmer, skim any scum that rises to the top. Dip the spider into a bowl of water and shake off the excess between skims to keep it clean.

The jam will look very thick and glossy when it's close to done, and sometimes you'll see waxy patches on the surface. The temperature should reach 216°F (102°C), about 25 minutes. When the jam is a few degrees from this temperature, remove from the heat and perform a plate test.

Spoon a little of the jam onto a frozen saucer. Put the plate back in the freezer for 1 minute, then slide a finger through the jam. It's done when it parts and you see a strip of clean plate. If it isn't set, return the pot to the heat, stir constantly, and test again after 1 or 2 minutes.

To Sqirl away your jam, see pages 16–21.

For peaches, nectarines, plums, apricots—I'm always looking for the right balance of sugar and acidity. I want the rich, sweet flavor of nectarine but also the tart notes that I need. The texture of the flesh should be melting, and ideally it would be a freestone fruit. Snow Queen nectarines have it all. We use the same recipe for Rose Diamond nectarines, which are also freestone.

Snow Queen nectarine jam Stone Fruit

Makes 8 half-pint jars

INGREDIENTS

2,672 g (5 lb 14 oz)	**nectarines**
1,171 g (5¾ cups plus 1 Tbsp)	**sugar** (50% of the weight of pitted nectarines)
46 g (3 Tbsp)	**lemon juice** (2% of the weight of pitted nectarines)

Put a few saucers in the freezer for your plate test.

Cut the nectarines in half. Twist out and discard the pits. Put the nectarine halves in a large bowl and smash them into pieces with your hands. You should have 2,342 g pitted nectarines.

If you have more or less nectarines, you can figure out the amount of sugar and lemon juice you need by using the following formula:

Grams of pitted nectarines × 0.50 = grams of sugar
Grams of pitted nectarines × 0.02 = grams of lemon juice

(You have the option to use the plumping technique here; see "Blending and Plumping" on page 14.)

Combine the nectarines with the sugar and lemon juice in your jamming pot. Cook over high heat, stirring frequently. Once the nectarines cook down and soften a bit, about 15 minutes, start smashing them with a potato masher. You want to keep smashing to break down any

large pieces. Using a spider or fine-mesh skimmer, skim any scum that rises to the top. Dip the spider into a bowl of water and shake off the excess between skims to keep it clean. The jam is finished when it's thickened and the temperature reaches 213°F (101°C), about 28 minutes total. When the jam is a few degrees from this temperature, remove from the heat and perform a plate test.

Spoon a little of the jam onto a frozen saucer. Put the plate back in the freezer for 1 minute, then slide a finger through the jam. It's done when it parts and you see a strip of clean plate. With nectarine jam, it might weep a little and that's okay. It should definitely part and not seep back together, though. If it isn't set, return the pot to the heat, stir constantly, and test again after 1 or 2 minutes

Stone Fruit

At Andy's Orchard in Morgan Hill, California—the variety of stone fruit here is dizzying. It's frenzy-making fruit whenever the summer crop arrives at the Santa Monica Farmers Market.

Peach season is a procession of varieties that span June to September at the L.A. markets. Mixing varieties is almost always a good idea—you get different but complementary flavors and textures. We marry June Lady and Rich Lady—two yellow peaches that are full-flavored, with firm but melting flesh (one's clingstone and the other's semi-freestone). Two ladies are better than one. Because peaches are sweet, we use as little sugar as possible; this means the jam will be less firm, a little looser, and it's not going to keep as long as a preserve with more sugar.

June and Rich Lady peach jam Stone Fruit

Makes 8 half-pint jars

INGREDIENTS

½ Tbsp	salt
3,088 g (6 lb 13 oz)	peaches
1,250 g (6¼ cups)	sugar (50% of the weight of pitted and peeled peaches)
50 g (3 Tbsp plus 1 tsp)	lemon juice (2% of the weight of pitted and peeled peaches)

Prepare your plate test by putting a few saucers in the freezer.

Bring a pot of water with the salt to a boil. Meanwhile, prepare an ice bath by filling a large bowl with ice and set aside.

Score the peaches with a sharp knife: Start at the pointed end of the peach and score an X that goes all the way around the circumference of the peach, being careful not to cut too deeply into the flesh.

Boil the peaches for 30 seconds and use a skimmer to transfer the peaches to the ice bath for 10 to 15 seconds. Remove the skins, using your fingers, and discard. Cut the peaches in half. Remove the pits, making sure the halves are totally cleaned of all parts of the seed. You should have 2,500 g pitted and peeled peaches.

If you have more or less than 2,500 g, you can figure out how much sugar and lemon juice you need by using the following formula:

Grams of pitted and peeled peaches × 0.50 = grams of sugar
Grams of pitted and peeled peaches × 0.02 = grams of lemon juice

Put the peach halves in a large bowl and smash the fruit with your hands. (You have the option to use the plumping technique here; see "Blending and Plumping" on page 14.) Combine the peaches with the sugar and lemon juice in your jamming pot. Cook over high heat, stirring frequently. Once the peaches cook down and soften a bit, about 20 minutes, start smashing them with a potato masher. You want to keep smashing to break down any large pieces—though you'll still have some chunks. Using a spider or fine-mesh skimmer, skim any scum that rises to the top. Dip the spider into a bowl of water and shake off the excess between skims to keep it clean. The jam is finished when it's thickened and the temperature reaches 211°F (99°C), about 35 minutes total. When the jam is a few degrees from this temperature, remove from the heat and perform a plate test.

Spoon a little of the jam onto a frozen saucer. Put the plate back in the freezer for 1 minute, then slide a finger through the jam. It's done when it parts and you see a strip of clean plate. It might weep a little and that's okay. It should definitely part and not seep back together, though. If it isn't set, return the pot to the heat, stir constantly, and test again after 1 or 2 minutes.

To Sqirl away your jam, see pages 16–21.

Variations:
Elberta peach jam with lemon verbena

David "Mas" Masumoto, an organic peach and grape farmer outside of Fresno, preserved old heirloom varieties of peaches such as Suncrest and Fay Elberta at a time when big buyers wanted nothing to do with them (not a popular color, too delicate for shipping, etc.), despite their flavor. In large part thanks to Mas and his adopt-a-tree program, we live in a world of more-nuanced peaches.

Put 11 g (1 cup) fresh lemon verbena leaves in a cheesecloth sachet tied with kitchen string. Add it to your jamming pot along with the peaches, sugar, and lemon juice. A few degrees before the temperature reaches 211°F (99°C), remove the jam from the heat. Remove the cheesecloth sachet, using tongs to squeeze out any excess liquid, and discard. This is a good time for a plate test.

Silver Logan peach jam with sumac

Silver Logan at its best is the ne plus ultra of white peaches, the peer of Snow Queen nectarines. It has milky white skin blushed with crimson. It's a freestone fruit, dense and buttery, with a balance of sweetness and acidity and a honey aroma.

When the jam's temperature is a few degrees from 211°F (99°C), remove from the heat and stir in 1½ Tbsp sumac until thoroughly combined.

ELEPHANT HEART PLUM JAM

What's not to love about the Elephant Heart plum? It has an endearing name, the speckled skin, the ombre red flesh, and the luscious, not-too-sweet flavor. This jam is all of the fruit's charm concentrated into a deep ruby preserve.

Makes 8 half-pint jars

INGREDIENTS

2,300 grams (5 lb 1 oz)	**Elephant Heart plums**
1,100 g (5½ cups)	**sugar** (50% of the weight of pitted plums)
65 g (1/4 cup plus 1 tsp)	**lemon juice** 3% of the weight of pitted plums)

Cut each plum in half and remove the pit. Cut the fruit into ½-inch slices. Weigh the fruit: You should have 2,200 g plum slices.

If you have more or less than 2,200 g plums, you can figure out how much sugar and lemon juice you need by using the following formula:

Grams of pitted plums × 0.50 = grams of sugar
Grams of pitted plums × 0.03 = grams of lemon juice

Combine the plums, sugar, and lemon juice in a jamming pot. (You have the option of using the plumping technique here; see "Blending and Plumping" on page 14.)

Cook over high heat, stirring frequently with a heatproof spatula. Bring the mixture to a boil (this will take about 10 minutes), being careful of overflowing, then reduce the heat to low. Using a spider or fine-mesh skimmer, skim any scum that rises to the top. Dip the spider into a bowl of water and shake off the excess between skims to keep it clean.

Smash the plums with a potato masher or whisk as they're cooking. You want to break up the fruit so that it melds into the mixture, but it will still be fairly chunky and have small pieces of skin.

Increase the heat to medium and continue to stir frequently. The jam is finished when the bubbles are smaller, the mixture has reduced by about a third, and the temperature reaches 218°F (103°C). When the jam is a few degrees from this temperature, remove from the heat and perform a plate test.

Spoon a little of the jam onto a frozen saucer. Put the plate back in the freezer for 1 minute, then slide a finger through the jam. It's done when it parts and you see a strip of clean plate. If it isn't set, return the pot to the heat, stir constantly, and test again after 1 or 2 minutes.

To Sqirl away your jam, see pages 16–21.

Elephant Heart plum jam Stone Fruit

Santa Rosas are a true California plum bred by the famed horticulturist Luther Burbank at his plant research center in Santa Rosa. Its fruit has a deep, rich flavor and the skin has a hint of tartness for a perfect balance. It's also beautiful—reddish-purple on the outside and golden amber on the inside.

Santa Rosa plum jam with flowering thyme Stone Fruit

Makes 8 half-pint jars

INGREDIENTS

3,000 g (6 lb 10 oz)   **Santa Rosa plums**
1,890 g (6 cups plus scant ½ cup)   **sugar** (70% of the weight of plums)
54 g (3 Tbsp plus 2 tsp)   **lemon juice** (2% of the weight of plums)
a few sprigs   **fresh flowering thyme**

Put a few saucers in the freezer for your plate test.

To remove the pits from the plums—because they're very soft when ripe—we just squeeze them over a large bowl with our hands. Let the fruit and skins fall into the bowl and discard the pits. You should have 2,700 g fruit and skins.

If you have more or less than 2,700 g plums, you can figure out how much sugar and lemon juice you need by using the following formula:

Grams of pitted plums × 0.70 = grams of sugar
Grams of pitted and peeled plums × 0.02 = grams of lemon juice

(You have the option to use the plumping technique here; see "Blending and Plumping" on page 14.)

Combine the plums with the sugar and lemon juice in your jamming pot. Tie a few sprigs of flowering thyme in a cheesecloth sachet and drop it in the pot.

Cook over high heat, stirring frequently with a heatproof spatula. The ripe plums are really juicy, so you'll be cooking off a lot of moisture and you'll see some pretty big bubbles. Using a spider or fine-mesh skimmer, skim any scum that rises to the top. Dip the spider into a bowl of water and shake off the excess between skims to keep it clean.

The jam is finished when it's thickened, the bubbles are smaller, and the temperature reaches 219°F (103°C), 45 to 50 minutes. When the jam is a few degrees from this temperature, remove from the heat. Remove the cheesecloth sachet with tongs, squeezing the bag over the pot to extract any liquid. Discard the sachet. Give the jam a stir. This is a good time for a plate test.

Spoon a little of the jam onto a frozen saucer. Put the plate back in the freezer for 1 minute, then slide a finger through the jam. It's done when it parts and you see a strip of clean plate. It might weep a little and that's okay. It should definitely part and not seep back together, though. If it isn't set, return the pot to the heat, stir constantly, and test again after 1 or 2 minutes.

To Sqirl away your jam, see pages 16–21.

There is some clingstone fruit too extraordinary to pass up: The Santa Rosa plum is one of them.

Jonathan Borofsky's "Molecule Man" sculpture, with plum   Stone Fruit

Jonathan Borofsky's "Molecule Man" sculpture, with plum   Stone Fruit

MIRABELLE PLUM JAM

Golden yellow Mirabelles, native to Lorraine in eastern France, show up in California between late July and September—a fairly short window, so we try to take full advantage of these treasures. They are little flavor bombs that are very sweet. It's an iconic French plum that traditionally has been used for jams. So we honor its place in the canon of fruit for preserves.

Mirabelle plum jam Stone Fruit

Makes 8 half-pint jars

2,400 g (5 lb 5 oz)	**Mirabelle plums**
945 g (4¾ cups)	**sugar** (45% of the weight of pitted plums)
105 g (¼ cup plus 3 tsp)	**lemon juice** (5% of the weight of pitted plums)

Prepare your plate test by putting a few saucers in the freezer.

Cut each plum in half, remove the pit, and cut in half again. Weigh the fruit: You should have 2,100 g pitted plums.

If you have more or less than 2,100 g plums, you can figure out how much sugar and lemon juice you need by using the following formula:

Grams of pitted plums × 0.45 = grams of sugar
Grams of pitted plums × 0.05 = grams of lemon juice

Put the fruit in a blender and puree until smooth (you'll still see flecks of plum skin). Transfer to your jamming pot and add the sugar and lemon juice. (You have the option of using the plumping technique here; see "Blending and Plumping" on page 14.)

Cook over high heat, stirring frequently with a heatproof spatula. You'll see some pretty big bubbles once it's boiling, after about 10 minutes. Be careful of overflowing. Reduce the heat to low. Using a spider or fine-mesh skimmer, skim any scum that rises to the top. Dip the spider into a bowl of water and shake off the excess between skims to keep it clean. You'll be skimming quite a lot.

Increase the heat to medium and continue to stir frequently. The jam is finished when the bubbles are smaller, the mixture has reduced by about a third, and the temperature reaches 213°F (101°C), about 20 minutes total. When the jam is a few degrees from this temperature, remove from the heat and perform a plate test.

Spoon a little of the jam onto a frozen saucer. Put the plate back in the freezer for 1 minute, then slide a finger through the jam. It's done when it parts and you see a strip of clean plate. If it isn't set, return the pot to the heat, stir constantly, and test again after 1 or 2 minutes.

To Sqirl away your jam, see pages 16–21.

DAMSON PLUM CHEESE

It was a revelation when I saw inky purple Damson plum cheese, or fruit paste, at Neal's Yard in London. I bought a piece to go with my Stichelton cheese, and I was so blown away that I had to figure out how to make it.

Damson plum cheese Stone Fruit

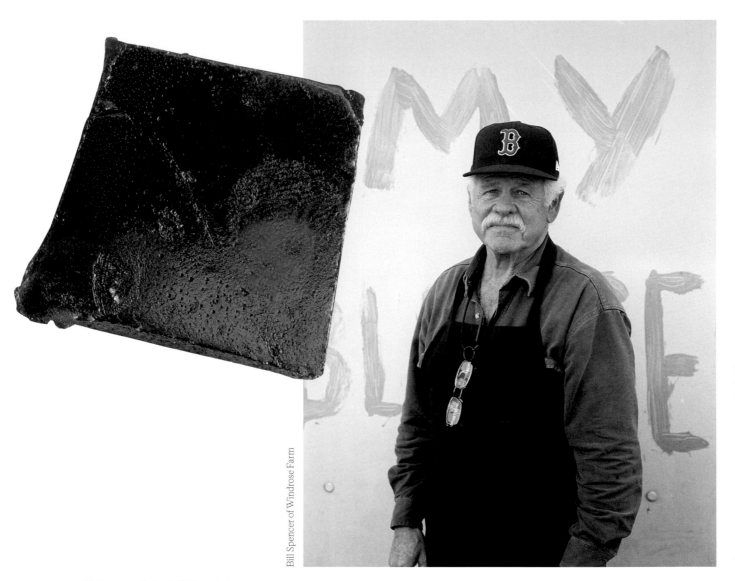

Bill Spencer of Windrose Farm

Makes one 8-inch (20-cm) square pan

INGREDIENTS

1,000 g (2 lb 3 oz)   **Damson plums**
575 g (2¾ cups plus 2 Tbsp)   **sugar** (75% of the weight of plum pulp)
30 g (2 Tbsp)   **lemon juice** (4% of the weight of plum pulp)

Put the plums and 118 g (½ cup) water in a heavy-bottom pot and cover it with a lid. Bring to a boil (this happens quickly) and then reduce to a simmer and cook until soft, 45 minutes to 1 hour. Remove from the heat and let cool slightly.

Carefully press the plums and their liquid through a food mill, watching out for pits. Alternatively, you can push this through a sieve. With the food mill, you'll probably need to remove the basket and use a wooden spoon and your hands to push through all of the pulp because the pits might get in the way. Discard the pits.

Weigh the plum pulp; you should have 768 g pulp. If you have more or less, you can figure out how much sugar and lemon juice you need with the following formula:

Grams of plum pulp × 0.75 = grams of sugar
Grams of plum pulp × 0.04 = grams of lemon juice

Line an 8-inch (20 cm) square baking pan with plastic wrap and set aside.

Put the plump pulp, sugar, and lemon juice in your jamming pot and bring to a boil over high heat. Reduce to a simmer and cook, stirring frequently with a heatproof spatula, until the mixture is very thick and has large, slow bubbles coming up from the bottom of the pot. The Damson cheese will be a shade deeper in color. When stirring, run a spatula across the bottom of the pot. If the gap is very slowly filled, the Damson cheese is ready.

Pour the mixture into your lined baking pan and press plastic wrap directly on top of the cheese so it doesn't form a skin. As it cools, it will continue to firm up. Serve with your favorite cheeses. Store covered in plastic wrap at room temperature for up to 1 month.

PLUM CHUTNEY

When we opened Sqirl this was on our original menu: plum chutney on brioche toast with San Andreas sheep's milk cheese. You could upgrade to add a fried duck egg. It hit all the sweet-spicy-savory notes—a nice balance to all the jams on the menu.

Plum chutney Stone Fruit

Makes about 10 half-pint jars

INGREDIENTS

2,500 g	**whole plums**
1,575 g (7¾ cups plus 1 Tbsp)	**sugar** (70% of the weight of quartered plums)
250 g (1 cup)	**distilled white vinegar** (11% of the weight of quartered plums)
113 g (½ cup)	**apple cider vinegar** (5% of the weight of quartered plums)
25 g (1½ Tbsp)	**fine sea salt** (1.3% of the weight of quartered plums)
30 g (2 Tbsp)	**yellow mustard seeds** (1.3% of the weight of quartered plums)
500 g	**chopped yellow onions** (about 2 medium onions) (22% of the weight of quartered plums)
	2 cloves garlic, finely grated with a rasp-style grater

Remove the stems and cut the plums into quarters and discard the pits. You should have about 2,250 g quartered plums.

If you have more or less than 2,250 g, you can figure out how much sugar, white vinegar, cider vinegar, salt, yellow mustard seeds, and onions you need with the following formula and adjust garlic to taste:

Grams of quartered plums x 0.70 = grams of sugar
Grams of quartered plums x 0.11 = grams of distilled white vinegar
Grams of quartered plums x 0.05 = grams of apple cider vinegar
Grams of quartered plums x 0.013 = grams of fine sea salt
Grams of quartered plums x 0.013 = grams of mustard seeds
Grams of quartered plums x 0.22 = grams of chopped yellow onions

Put the plums, sugar, white vinegar, cider vinegar, and salt in a large pot and bring to a boil, stirring and scraping the bottom of the pot with a heatproof spatula so the sugars don't burn.

Once it's boiling, reduce the heat to medium. Add the mustard seeds, onions, and garlic. Using a spider or fine-mesh skimmer, skim the scum that rises to the top, being careful not to remove the spices and aromatics. Dip the spider into a bowl of water and shake off the excess between skims to keep it clean.

After you skim any scum from the top, turn the heat back up to medium-high to high and continue to cook until the temperature reaches 218°F (103°C); this will take about 1 hour of total cooking time. When the chutney nears this temperature, remove from the heat and perform a plate test.

Spoon a little of the chutney onto a frozen saucer. Put the plate back in the freezer for 1 minute, then slide a finger through the chutney. It's done when it parts and you see a strip of clean plate. If it isn't set, return the pot to the heat, stir constantly, and test again after 1 or 2 minutes.

To Sqirl away your chutney, see pages 16–21.

Plum chutney Stone Fruit

This page: Mark di Suvero, 1982 Shoshone, Bunker Hill, Los Angeles Opposite: D'Agen French prune plums—not what we typically use to make jam, but they're great fresh and as dried prunes.

Stone Fruit

Stone Fruit

REINE CLAUDE JAM

Reine Claude plums are celebrated greengages, one of the most delicious stone fruit around, extra rich and lovely to eat whole (if I were to eat whole fruit). They also make excellent preserves—sweet, but with counterbalancing acidity and a gorgeous golden-green color.

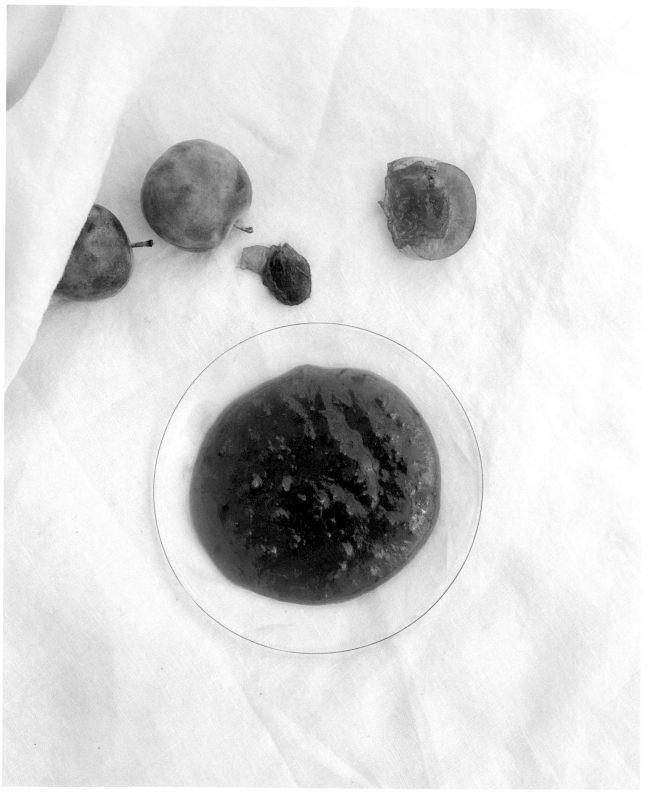

Makes about 7 half-pint jars

INGREDIENTS

2,300 g (5 lb 1 oz)	**whole Reine Claude plums**
945 g (4¾ cups)	**sugar** (45% of the weight of pitted plums)
63 g (¼ cup)	**lemon juice** (3% of the weight of pitted plums)

Cut each plum in half, remove the pit. Cut each half into three wedges. Weigh the fruit: You should have 2,100 g pitted plums.

If you have more or less than 2,100 g plums, you can figure out how much sugar and lemon juice you need by using the following formula:

Grams of pitted plums × 0.50 = grams of sugar
Grams of pitted plums × 0.02 = grams of lemon juice

Put the plums in a blender and puree. Transfer to your jamming pot and add the sugar and lemon juice. (You have the option of using the plumping technique here; see "Blending and Plumping" on page 14.)

Cook over high heat, stirring frequently with a heatproof spatula. The ripe plums are juicy, so you'll be cooking off a lot of moisture and you'll see some pretty big bubbles once it's boiling, after about 10 minutes. Be careful of overflowing. Reduce the heat to low. Using a spider or fine-mesh skimmer, skim any scum that rises to the top. Dip the spider into a bowl of water and shake off the excess between skims to keep it clean.

Increase the heat to medium and continue to stir frequently. The jam is finished when the bubbles are smaller, the mixture has reduced by about a third, and the temperature reaches 219°F (103°C), about 20 minutes total. When the jam is a few degrees from this temperature, remove from the heat and perform a plate test.

Spoon a little of the jam onto a frozen saucer. Put the plate back in the freezer for 1 minute, then slide a finger through the jam. It's done when it parts and you see a strip of clean plate. If it isn't set, return the pot to the heat, stir constantly, and test again after 1 or 2 minutes.

To Sqirl away your jam, see pages 16–21.

HONEY PUNCH PLUOT JAM

I think of pluots as more plum than apricot and apriums as more apricot than plum—they each have characteristics of both. Honey Punch pluots are up to 75% plum and have a beautiful smooth skin that's deep red and speckled, sometimes with a grayish-purple bloom. The interior is golden and, like the name suggests, honeyed. Find any pluot you love for this jam.

Makes 8 half-pint jars

INGREDIENTS

3,000 g (6 lb 10 oz) **Honey Punch pluots**
1,620 g (8 cups plus 1½ Tbsp) **sugar** (60% of the weight of pitted pluots)
108 g (2½ Tbsp) **lemon juice** (4% of the weight of pitted pluots)

To remove the pits from the pluots, squeeze the fruit over a large bowl with your hands. Let the fruit and skins fall into the bowl and discard the seeds. You should have 2,700 g fruit and skins.

If you have more or less than 2,700 g pluots, you can figure out how much sugar and lemon juice you need by using the following formula:

Grams of pitted pluots × 0.60 = grams of sugar
Grams of pitted and peeled pluots × 0.04 = grams of lemon juice

Combine the plums with the sugar and lemon juice in your jamming pot. (Or, you also have the option to use the plumping technique here; see "Blending and Plumping" on page 14.) Cook over high heat, stirring frequently with a heatproof spatula. The ripe pluots are juicy, so you'll be cooking off a lot of moisture and you'll see some pretty big bubbles. Using a spider or fine-mesh skimmer, skim any scum that rises to the top. Dip the spider into a bowl of water and shake off the excess between skims to keep it clean.

The jam is finished when it's thickened, the bubbles are smaller, and the temperature reaches 217°F (103°C), about 35 minutes. When the jam is a few degrees from this temperature, remove from the heat and perform a plate test.

Spoon a little of the jam onto a frozen saucer. Put the plate back in the freezer for 1 minute, then slide a finger through the jam. It's done when it parts and you see a strip of clean plate. It might weep a little and that's okay. It should definitely part and not seep back together, though. If it isn't set, return the pot to the heat, stir constantly, and test again after 1 or 2 minutes.

To Sqirl away your jam, see pages 16–21.

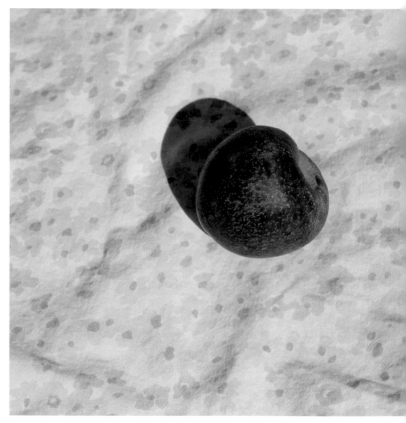

The Honey Punch pluot is on the sweeter side and it's clingstone, but true to its name, the fruit tastes of delicious honey.

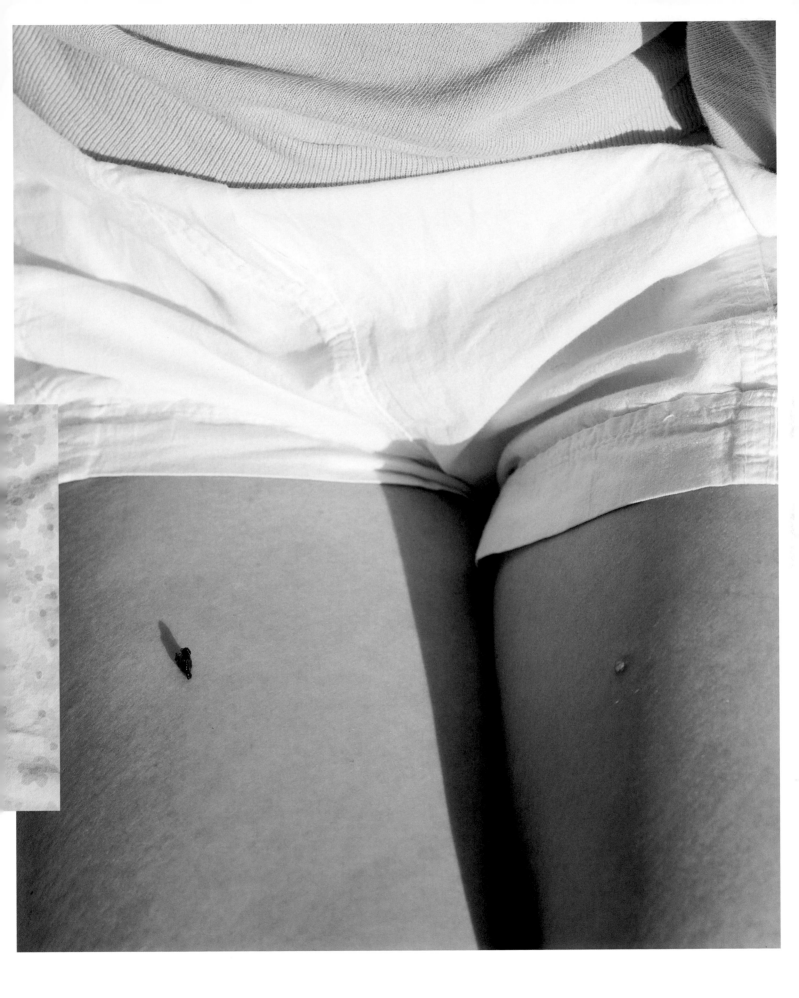

Honey Punch pluot jam Stone Fruit

This cookie is special to me because I grew up going to temple and Purim carnivals—and truly enjoyed the holiday not because I had any deep understanding of it but because I got to eat Haman's hats. The hat-shaped cookies can be filled with any kind of jam. But my favorite is apricot. Nothing can replace that (though a good poppy seed hamantaschen is a close second).

Makes 16 to 20 (3-inch/7.5 cm) cookies

INGREDIENTS

312 g (2½ cups)	**all-purpose flour**
34 g (¼ cup)	**whole wheat flour**
1½ tsp	**baking powder**
150 g (¾ cup)	**sugar**
100 g (½ cup)	**canola oil**
2	**whole large eggs**
1	**egg yolk**
1 Tbsp	**orange juice**
1 tsp	**vanilla extract**
1 tsp	**salt**
160 to 200 g (about ½ cup)	**jam** (it's best to use a thicker jam because a looser jam will be harder to work with)
	sugar for sprinkling

Whisk together the flours and baking powder until combined.

In a stand mixer fitted with the paddle attachment, beat the sugar, oil, 1 of the whole eggs, the egg yolk, orange juice, vanilla, and salt on medium speed until smooth and shiny, about 2 minutes.

Turn the mixer off and add the flour and baking powder mixture. Turn the mixer on and off to mix just until incorporated, scraping down the bowl as needed. Divide the dough in half, shape each portion into a disk, and wrap in plastic wrap. Refrigerate for 1 hour.

Remove one disk of dough from the refrigerator. Roll it between two pieces of floured parchment paper to ⅛ inch (3 mm) thick. Repeat with the other half. Return the dough, leaving it between the parchment paper, to the refrigerator and chill for 2 hours.

Remove the dough from the refrigerator. Peel the parchment off both sides of the dough so that the parchment doesn't stick to the dough when cutting out the cookies. Place the dough back on one of the pieces of parchment on a cutting board or baking sheet. Using a 3-inch (7.5 cm) round cookie cutter, cut the dough into circles. Form the scraps into a disk, wrap it in plastic, and put it in the refrigerator while you're shaping your cookies. You can roll out the scraps one more time.

Heat the oven to 325°F. Line two baking sheets with parchment paper. Place up to 12 cookie rounds per sheet. If the dough starts to get soft, transfer it back to the refrigerator to chill for 10 minutes. Put 1 teaspoon jam in the center of each cookie and pinch the dough together in three places, evenly spaced apart along the edges, to form three points. Repeat with all of the dough, including the scraps. Let the cookies chill in the refrigerator for 10 minutes after forming.

Beat the remaining egg in a small bowl with a splash of water. Remove the cookies from the refrigerator, brush with egg wash, and sprinkle with sugar. Bake until the edges are light brown, 15 to 17 minutes, rotating halfway through for even baking. Remove from the oven and let cool on a rack. Store in an airtight container at room temperature for up to 5 days.

Hamantaschen Stone Fruit

FIGS

128–135

Fig jam with red wine[128]

Figs

Fig jam is always on a cheese plate, and wherever there's a cheese plate, you're always drinking wine with it. So fig jam and red wine just seemed to go together. A jug of wine, a basket of figs … sounds like jam to me. I started making it with Mourvèdre from La Clarine Farm. A nice deep red, made from a bold grape that's not afraid of heat. I love Mission figs because they're iconic to California and a great jamming fig.

Makes 9 half-pint jars

INGIREDIENTS

2,400 g (5 lbs 5 oz)	**Mission figs**
1,150 g (5¾ cups)	**sugar** (50% of the weight of trimmed figs)
69 g (¼ cup plus 2 tsp)	**lemon juice** (3% of the weight of trimmed figs)
161 g (⅔ cup)	**red wine** (7% of the weight of trimmed figs)

Prepare your plate test by putting a few saucers in the freezer.

Trim and discard the stem ends of the figs. You should have 2,300 g trimmed figs. If you have more or less than 2,300 g trimmed figs, you can figure out how much sugar, lemon juice, and wine you need by using the following formula:

Grams of trimmed figs × 0.50 = grams of sugar
Grams of trimmed figs × 0.03 = grams of lemon juice
Grams of trimmed figs × 0.07 = grams of wine

Put about two-thirds of the figs in a blender and blend until pureed. Cut the remaining of the figs into small wedges (6 wedges per fig). (You have the option to use the plumping technique here; see "Blending and Plumping" on page 14.)

Combine the pureed figs, fig wedges, sugar, and lemon juice in your jamming pot and cook over high heat. Use a heatproof spatula to stir, scraping the bottom of the pot so the sugars don't caramelize. With a spider or fine-mesh skimmer, skim any scum from the surface. Dip the spider into a bowl of water and shake off the excess between skims to keep it clean. The jam is finished when it's thickened, the fig wedges have started to melt (there will still be small chunks), and the mixture reaches a temperature of 208°F (99°C), about 23 minutes. You might also notice waxy patches on the surface of the jam. A few degrees before the jam reaches 208°F, add the wine. Cook for an additional 3 minutes so that the wine becomes incorporated into the jam. Remove from the heat and perform a plate test.

Spoon a little of the jam onto a frozen saucer. Put the plate back in the freezer for 1 minute, then slide a finger through the jam. It's done when it parts and you see a strip of clean plate. If it isn't set, return the pot to the heat, stir constantly, and test again after 1 or 2 minutes.

To Sqirl away your jam, see pages 16–21.

Fig jam (made with a jug of wine on hand) over an open fire at Jasud Estate, Diamond Mountain, California

Fig jam with red wine Figs

Fig jam with red wine Figs

Fig jam with red wine Figs

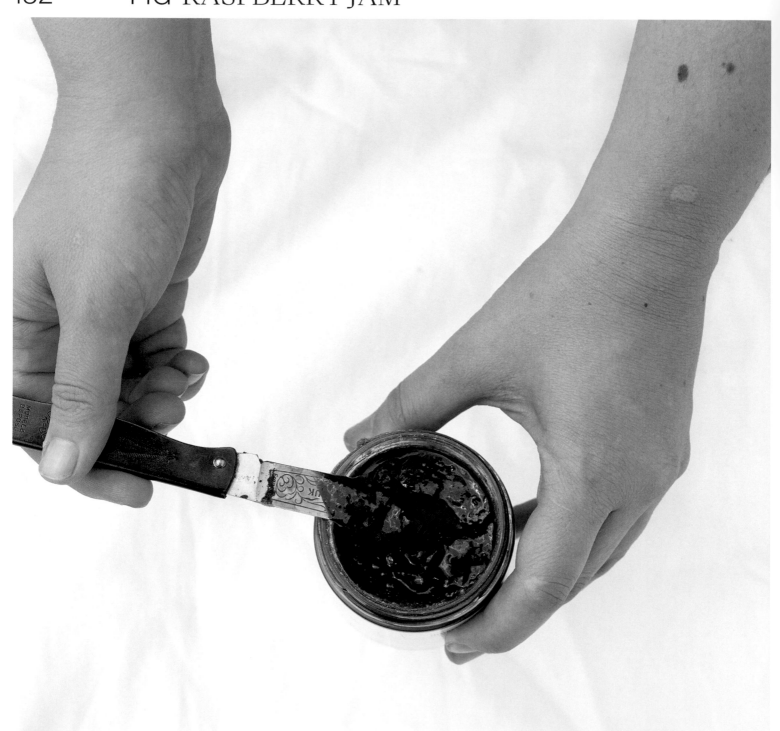

Figs in some ways have a very similar consistency to berries when they cook. Bright, sweet-tart raspberries are delicious with figs. But it would also be interesting to try another berry with this. Trade out the raspberry for blackberries. Figs have a lot of pectin, so you could get similar results. Or even try plums. Play around.

Makes 8 half-pint jars

INGIREDIENTS

1,230 g (2 lbs 12 oz)	**Mission figs**
510 g (1 lb 2 oz)	**raspberries**
935 g (4⅔ cups)	**sugar** (55% of the weight of trimmed figs plus raspberries)
51 g (3 Tbsp plus 1 tsp)	**lemon juice** (3% of the weight of trimmed figs plus raspberries)

Prepare your plate test by putting a few saucers in the freezer.

Trim and discard the stem ends of the figs. You should have 1,190 g trimmed figs.

If you have more or less than 1,190 g trimmed figs and 510 g raspberries (a mixture of 70% figs and 30% raspberries), you can figure out how much sugar and lemon juice you need by using the following formula:

Grams of trimmed figs plus raspberries x 0.55 = grams of sugar
Grams of trimmed figs plus raspberries x 0.03 = grams of lemon juice

Puree the figs and raspberries in a blender until coarsely pureed. (Alternatively, cut half of the figs into small wedges and put half of the berries in a large bowl and crush them with your hands; puree the rest and combine the puree with the crushed fruit. You also have the option to use the plumping technique here; see "Blending and Plumping" on page 14.)

Combine the figs and raspberries, sugar, and lemon juice in your jamming pot and cook over high heat. Use a heatproof spatula to stir, scraping the bottom of the pot so the sugars don't caramelize. With a spider or fine-mesh skimmer, skim any scum from the surface. Dip the spider into a bowl of water and shake off the excess between skims to keep it clean. The jam is finished when it's thickened and the mixture reaches a temperature of 208°F (98°C), about 19 minutes. You might also notice waxy patches on the surface of the jam. A few degrees before the temperature reaches 208°F, remove from the heat and perform a plate test.

Spoon a little of the jam onto a frozen saucer. Put the plate back in the freezer for 1 minute, then slide a finger through the jam. It's done when it parts and you see a strip of clean plate. If it isn't set, return to the heat, stir constantly, and test again after 1 or 2 minutes.

To Sqirl away your jam, see pages 16–21.

Fig–Raspberry Jam Figs

Fig–Raspberry Jam Figs

TOMATOES

Tomato jam with saffron and caraway[138], Tomato jam with tamarind and mint[140], Tomato jam sandwich[143]

Tomatoes

Makes 10 half-pint jars

INGIREDIENTS

2,600 g (6 lb 5 oz)	**tomatoes**
750 g (3¾ cups)	**sugar** (30% of the weight of trimmed tomatoes)
17.5 g (1 Tbsp plus 1 tsp)	**Maldon sea salt** (0.7% of the weight of trimmed tomatoes)
70 g (¼ cup plus ½ Tbsp)	**white vinegar** (2.8% of the weight of pitted cherries)
Pinch	**saffron threads**
1 tsp	**toasted ground caraway**

To prepare your plate test, put a few saucers in the freezer.

Cut the tomatoes in half and trim the stem ends. You should have 2,500 g trimmed tomatoes. If you have more or less tomatoes, you can figure out how much sugar, salt, and vinegar juice you need by using the following formula:

Grams of trimmed tomatoes × 0.30 = grams of sugar
Grams of trimmed tomatoes × 0.007 = grams of salt
Grams of trimmed tomatoes × 0.028 = grams of vinegar

Puree the tomatoes in the blender. Combine the tomato puree, sugar, salt, vinegar, and saffron in your jamming pot over high heat. Stir and skim as the tomato mixture cooks; there will be lots of skimming. Using a spider or fine-mesh skimmer to remove the scum that rises to the top. Dip the spider into a bowl of water and shake off the excess between skims to keep it clean.

Once the mixture starts boiling, 15 to 20 minutes, reduce the heat to medium. Keep skimming and continue to cook until the jam is thickened and reduced by about half and the temperature reaches 214°F (101°C), about 1 hour total.

A few degrees before the jam reaches 214°F (101°C), remove from the heat and stir in the caraway until combined. This is a good time to perform a plate test. Spoon a little of the jam onto a frozen saucer. Put the plate back in the freezer for 1 minute, then slide a finger through the jam. It's done when it parts and you see a strip of clean plate. If it isn't set, return to the heat, stir constantly, and test again after 1 or 2 minutes.

Tomato jam with saffron and caraway Tomatoes

Tomato jam with saffron and caraway Tomatoes

This version of tomato jam is a nod to Onda, the restaurant that I opened with Gabriela Cámara in Santa Monica. It's a tomato jam that blends our two perspectives.

Makes 4 half-pint jars

INGREDIENTS

1,770 g (3 lb 14 oz)	**whole tomatoes**
100 g (about ¼ cup)	**tamarind paste** (6% of the weight of tomato puree)
525 (2⅔ cups)	**sugar** (30% of the weight of tomato puree)
14 g (about 1 Tbsp)	**Maldon sea salt** (0.8% of the weight of tomato puree)
50 g (3½ Tbsp)	**distilled white vinegar** (2.9% of the weight of tomato puree)
	Heavy pinch of chile flakes (optional)
40 g (about 2 cups)	**fresh mint leaves** (2.3% of the weight of tomato puree)

Prepare your plate test by putting a few saucers in the freezer.

Trim the tomatoes and cut them into large chunks. Puree the tomatoes in a blender until completely smooth. You should have 1,750 g tomato puree.

If you have more or less than 1,750 g, you can figure out how much tamarind, sugar, salt, vinegar, and mint you need by using the following formula:

$$\text{Grams of tomato puree} \times 0.06 = \text{grams of tamarind}$$
$$\text{Grams of tomato puree} \times 0.30 = \text{grams of sugar}$$
$$\text{Grams of tomato puree} \times 0.08 = \text{grams of salt}$$
$$\text{Grams of tomato puree} \times 0.029 = \text{grams of distilled white vinegar}$$
$$\text{Grams of tomato puree} \times 0.023 = \text{grams of fresh mint leaves}$$

Put the tomato puree in a large pot with the tamarind, sugar, salt, vinegar and chile flakes, if using. Put the mint in a sachet of cheesecloth tied with kitchen string and add it to the pot. Bring it to a boil then reduce the heat to medium. Using a spider or fine-mesh skimmer, skim any scum (there won't be a lot) that rises to the top. Dip the spider into a bowl of water and shake off the excess between skims to keep it clean.

Continue to cook over medium heat until the tomato jam is very glossy and reduced by about two-thirds (a lot of liquid will cook off), and the temperature reaches 216°F (102°C). A few degrees before it reaches this temperature, remove the jam from the heat. Remove the cheesecloth sachet, using tongs to squeeze out any excess liquid, and discard. This is a good time for a plate test.

Spoon a little of the jam onto a frozen saucer. Put the plate back in the freezer for 1 minute, then slide a finger through the jam. It's done when it parts and you see a strip of clean plate. It might weep a little, and that's okay. It should definitely part and not seep back together, though. If it isn't set, return the pot to the heat, stir constantly, and test again after 1 or 2 minutes.

To Sqirl away your marmalade, see pages 16–21.

Tomatoes with tamarind and mint Tomatoes

Tomatoes with tamarind and mint Tomatoes

Tomato jam sandwich Tomatoes

TOMATO JAM SANDWICH

This is my favorite sandwich, smeared with savory-tart-sweet tomato jam and toasted with cheese until melty. With a bitter hint of fresh arugula, it hits all the right notes. You also can use the Shady Lady tomato and coriander jam from *Everything I Want to Eat*, pages 198–99.

Makes 1 sandwich

INGREDIENTS

1 small handful	**arugula**
30 g (2 Tbsp)	**lemon juice**
7-in piece	**baguette**
50 g (2½ Tbsp)	**tomato jam with saffron and caraway** (page 138)
50 g (3½ Tbsp)	**shredded cheddar cheese**
15 g (1 Tbsp)	**melted unsalted butter**

Toss the arugula with the lemon juice and set aside.

Put the bread on a cutting board and split it in half horizontally. Open the two halves so that the soft interior part of the bread is facing up. Spread the jam on both pieces of bread, then top each piece with an even layer of cheese. Place the two pieces of cheese-topped bread on a small baking pan. Toast in the oven until the cheese is melted, rotating halfway through cooking for even melting, about 4 minutes total. Remove from the oven.

Close the sandwich and brush each outer side with the melted butter, using a pastry brush.

Transfer the sandwich to a skillet over medium-high heat, place a piece of foil loosely over the top, and put a weight on it—another heavy skillet or a flat plate or board with a can of beans on top. You want to press the sandwich thoroughly. Cook until the underside is deep golden brown. Flip the sandwich, weight it again, and cook until the other side is deep golden brown.

Open the sandwich and place the arugula inside. Re-close the sandwich and serve immediately.

TROPICAL FRUITS
146–149

Mango–passion fruit jam[146], Guava jam[148]

Tropical Fruits

Tropical Fruits

MANGO–PASSION FRUIT JAM

This jam reminds me to take a break, go to the beach, put on a bikini, and get sand between my toes. It's a vacation in a jar.

Mango–passion fruit jam Tropical Fruits

Makes 7 half-pint jars

INGREDIENTS

907 g (2 lb)	**passion fruit**
1,928 g (4 lb 4 oz)	**mangos**
800 g (4 cups)	**sugar** (50% of the weight of passion fruit juice plus mango puree)
413 g (1¾ cups)	**apple pectin** (page 178) (25% of the weight of passion fruit juice plus mango puree)
45 g (3 Tbsp)	**lemon juice** (3% of the weight of passion fruit juice plus mango puree)

Prepare your plate test by putting a few saucers in the freezer.

Cut the passion fruit in half crosswise. Scoop out the pulp and put it in a blender. Pulse to break up the pulp and make it looser. Transfer to a mesh strainer and strain out the seeds. Set the juice aside and discard the seeds. You should have 286 g (1¼ cups) passion fruit juice.

Cut the fruit from the mango: Cut lengthwise along the two flat sides of the pit to get two "halves." Use a spoon to scoop all of the fruit away from the skin and discard the skin. Peel the skin from the remaining fruit around the pit and cut the fruit off the pit; discard the pit and skin. Put the fruit in a blender and puree until smooth. You should have 1,343 g (4½ cups) puree.

If you have more or less than 286 g passion fruit juice and 1,343 g mango puree (20% passion fruit juice and 80% mango puree), you can figure out how much sugar, apple pectin, and lemon juice you need by using the following formula:

Grams of passion fruit juice plus mango puree × 0.50 = grams of sugar
Grams of passion fruit juice plus mango puree × 0.25 = grams of apple pectin
Grams of passion fruit juice plus mango puree × 0.03 = grams of lemon juice

Put the passion fruit juice, mango puree, sugar, apple pectin, and lemon juice in your jamming pot over high heat. Use a heatproof spatula to stir, scraping the bottom of the pot so the sugars don't caramelize. With a spider or fine-mesh skimmer, skim any scum from the surface. Dip the spider into a bowl of water and shake off the excess between skims to keep it clean. Cook until the jam is thickened slightly, the mixture has small, vigorous bubbles, and the temperature reaches 218°F (103°C), 20 to 25 minutes. A few degrees before the jam reaches this temperature, remove from the heat and perform a plate test.

Spoon a little of the jam onto a frozen saucer. Put the plate back in the freezer for 1 minute, then slide a finger through the jam. It's done when it parts and you see a strip of clean saucer. If it isn't set, return the pot to the heat, stir frequently, and test after another minute.

To Sqirl away your marmalade see pages 16–21.

GUAVA JAM

Another beachy jam. I love everything about guava. If you use the pink-fleshed guavas, the color of the jam will be a deep rosy pink.

Guava jam Tropical Fruit

Makes 6 to 8 half-pint jars

INGREDIENTS

2,724 g (6 lb)	**guavas**
866 g (4⅓ cups)	**sugar** (55% of the weight of pureed guavas)
90 g (6 Tbsp)	**lemon juice** (6% of the weight of pureed guavas)

Prepare your plate test by putting a few saucers in the freezer.

Peel the guavas and discard the peel. Cut off the ends and discard. Transfer to a blender along with 590 g (2½ cups) water and blend until smooth. You might need to do this in batches. The puree will become smooth but the seeds should stay intact. Push the puree through a medium-mesh strainer and discard the seeds.

You should have 1,589 g (3 lb 8 oz) puree. If you have more or less, you can figure out how much sugar and lemon juice you need by using the following formula:

Grams of guava puree × 0.55 = grams of sugar
Grams of guava puree × 0.06 = grams of lemon juice

Combine the guava puree, sugar, and lemon juice in your jamming pot. Cook over high heat and use a heatproof spatula to stir, scraping the bottom of the pot so the sugars don't caramelize. With a spider or fine-mesh skimmer, skim any scum from the surface. Dip the spider into a bowl of water and shake off the excess between skims to keep it clean. As your jam gets closer to being set, you will start hearing a sizzling sound as you stir. Cook until the jam is thickened and glossy and the temperature reaches 221°F (105°C), 20 to 25 minutes. A few degrees before the jam reaches this temperature, remove from the heat and perform a plate test.

Spoon a little of the jam onto a frozen saucer. Put the plate back in the freezer for 1 minute, then slide a finger through the jam. It's done when it parts and you see a strip of clean saucer. If it isn't set, return the pot to the heat, stir frequently, and test after another minute.

To Sqirl away your jam, see pages 16–21.

MEDLARS
152–155

Medlar butter[152], Loquat butter[154]

Medlars

MEDLAR BUTTER

Medlars are a weird, rusty-brown fruit that look like giant rosehips (the medlar tree is in fact in the rose family). Like Hachiya persimmons, they have to be eaten very ripe (like almost rotten), and when they're very ripe, they have to be eaten right away. Or you can preserve them. They make a beautiful butter.

Medlars also make a pinkish-hued quince-like jelly, and David Lebovitz' version online is a popular recipe.

Medlar butter Medlars

INGREDIENTS

2,500 g (5½ lbs)	**ripe medlars**	
1,032 g (5 cups plus 2½ Tbsp)	**sugar** (43% of the weight of medlar puree)	
72 g (¼ cup plus 2 tsp)	**lemon juice** (3% of the weight of medlar puree)	

Prepare your plate test by putting a few saucers in the freezer.

Put the ripe medlars in a large pot and smash them with your hands. Add 8 cups of water and bring it to a boil. Once it boils, reduce to a simmer and cook the medlars for 20 minutes.

Place a large strainer (not one with fine holes) over a large bowl. Pour the medlars and their liquid into the strainer-lined bowl. Push the fruit through with a ladle. It will be a chunky puree. Weigh the puree; you should have 2,400 g.

If you have more or less puree, you can figure out how much sugar and lemon juice you need by using the following formula:

Grams of medlar puree × 0.43 = grams of sugar
Grams of guava puree × 0.03 = grams of lemon juice

Combine the puree, sugar, and lemon juice in your jamming pot. As it comes to a boil, stir with a heatproof spatula, scraping the bottom of the pot so the sugars don't caramelize. With a spider or fine-mesh skimmer, skim any scum from the surface. Dip the spider into a bowl of water and shake off the excess between skims to keep it clean.

It will bubble vigorously, so after 10 to 15 minutes reduce the heat to medium. Continue cooking until the mixture has thickened, reduced by about one-third, and the temperature reaches 215°F (102°C), about 30 minutes total.

A few degrees before it reaches this temperature, remove from the heat and perform a plate test. Spoon a little of the mixture onto a frozen saucer. Put the plate back in the freezer for 1 minute, then slide a finger through the butter. It's done when it parts and you see a strip of clean saucer. If it isn't set, return the pot to the heat, stir frequently, and test after another 1 to 2 minutes.

To Sqirl away your butter, see pages 16–21.

LOQUAT BUTTER

Loquat trees grow all over Los Angeles, and their yellow-orange fruit is abundant. There's so much fruit that most people don't even know what to do with it. Enter loquat butter. The fruit has to be ripe when picked (it doesn't ripen off the tree)—it should be yellow-orange, not greenish or pale yellow.

Loquat butter Medlars

Makes 7 half-pint jars

INGREDIENTS

2,510 g (5½ lbs)	**ripe loquats**
812 g (4 cups plus 1 Tbsp)	**sugar** (43% of the weight of loquat puree)
94.5 g (¼ cup plus 2 Tbsp plus 1 tsp)	**lemon juice** (5% of the weight of loquat puree)

Prepare your plate test by putting a few saucers in the freezer.

Tear the loquats open with your hands, removing and discarding the seeds, so that you have two halves for each fruit. Cut each half in half again. (You'll have about 1,550 g loquat fruit.)

Put the quartered loquats in a large pot and cover them with 6 cups water. Bring to a boil, covered, and cook until the fruit is soft, 30 minutes.

Transfer the loquat and water to a blender and blend until fairly smooth. Pass the mixture through a fine strainer, using a ladle to push the fruit through the openings of the strainer. It won't be completely smooth—you'll get some solids and the texture will be sort of like applesauce. Weigh the puree; you should have 1,890 g puree.

If you have more or less puree, you can figure out how much sugar and lemon juice you need by using the following formula:

Grams of loquat puree x 0.43 = grams of sugar
Grams of loquat puree x 0.05 = grams of lemon juice

Combine the loquat puree, sugar, and lemon juice in your jamming pot. As it comes to a boil, stir with a heatproof spatula, scraping the bottom of the pot so the sugars don't caramelize. With a spider or fine-mesh skimmer, skim any scum from the surface. Dip the spider into a bowl of water and shake off the excess between skims to keep it clean.

It will bubble vigorously, so after 10 to 15 minutes reduce the heat to medium. Continue cooking until the mixture has thickened and reduced by about one-third, and the temperature reaches 214°F (101°C), about 25 minutes total. It should come off your spatula as a single "sheet" of butter. A few degrees before it reaches this temperature, remove from the heat and perform a plate test.

Spoon a little of the mixture onto a frozen saucer. Put the plate back in the freezer for 1 minute, then slide a finger through the butter. It's done when it parts and you see a strip of clean saucer. If it isn't set, return the pot to the heat, stir frequently, and test after another 1 to 2 minutes.

To Sqirl away your butter, see pages 16–21.

CRANBERRIES & GRAPES

158–167

164

Cranberries and Grapes

Bourbon cranberry jam[158] Cranberry-apple butter[160] Concord grape jam[162] Scuppernong jam[166]

BOURBON CRANBERRY JAM

I moved to Boston to go to college and met Jensen Reems, who was from a third-generation cranberry-bog family in Massachusetts. I went to the farm for Thanksgiving, and I'd never experienced the family unit in such a loving way, and they were using all this food from the farm. His mom, who was in the fashion industry and lived in New York, cooked the entire meal. She made the cranberry sauce by just putting cranberries, sugar, and cinnamon on a baking sheet and then pouring Jack Daniels all over it when it was all disintegrating. I didn't know that cranberries could taste so good, that cranberry sauce could have this different life. It's the inspiration for this bourbon cranberry jam. I serve it every year at our Thanksgiving table.

Makes about 660 g (2¼ cups)

INGREDIENTS

453 g (1 lb)	**fresh or frozen cranberries, stemmed and rinsed**
453 g (1 lb)	**sugar**
½ tsp	**ground cinnamon**
120 g (½ cup)	**bourbon**

Combine the cranberries, sugar, and cinnamon in a large pot; cook over high heat for about 8 minutes, stirring constantly, until just about all the berries have burst. If you are using frozen berries, the mixture might yield liquid; you can cook that off for another minute or two. Remove from the heat.

Stir in the bourbon. Return to high heat, stirring constantly for 1 to 2 minutes, to let the bourbon cook off.

Let cool; the jam will thicken. Serve at room temperature.

Bourbon cranberry sauce Cranberries and Grapes

Bourbon cranberry sauce Cranberries and Grapes

CRANBERRY-APPLE BUTTER

Cranberries and apples make a delicious pie.
So why not make it a jam?

Cranberry-apple butter Cranberries and Grapes

Makes 9 half-pint jars

INGREDIENTS

2,000 g (4 lb 6 oz) **apples** (a soft variety such as Fuji)
600 g (1 lb 5 oz) **fresh or frozen cranberries, stemmed and rinsed**
1,200 g (6 cups) **sugar** (60% of the weight of apple puree plus cranberries)
60 g (¼ cup) **lemon juice** (3% of the weight of apple puree plus cranberries)

Prepare your plate test by putting a few saucers in the freezer.

Cut the apples into quarters and remove the cores. Put the apples in a large pot and cover with water. Bring the apples to a boil, then reduce the heat to a simmer. Simmer the apples, stirring once in a while so that they cook evenly, until fork tender, 35 to 40 minutes. Remove from the heat. Drain and discard the liquid.

Use a food mill to puree the apples (milling is faster while the fruit is still hot). By using a food mill you will remove the peels and get great texture. You should have 1,400 g apple puree—for a combined 2,000 g of apple puree and cranberries. (We use a combination of 70% apples and 30% cranberries for this recipe.) If you have more or less, you can figure out how much sugar and lemon juice you need by using the following formula:

Grams of apple puree plus cranberries × 0.60 = grams of sugar
Grams of apple puree plus cranberries × 0.03 = grams of lemon juice

Blend the cranberries in a blender with the apple puree and lemon juice.

Combine the apple-cranberry puree with the sugar in a jamming pot over high heat. As the apple butter cooks, stir frequently and when it's closer to setting, stir constantly with a heatproof spatula to prevent scorching. Be careful because apple butter will bubble not only vigorously but volcanically; lower the heat when necessary. Cook until thick and sludgy and the temperature reaches 208°F (98°C), about 20 minutes. When the apple butter nears this temperature, remove from the heat and perform a plate test.

Spoon a little of the apple butter onto a frozen saucer. It should puff up (like a raised mole) when it hits the cold plate. Look at the edges; the butter should not be seeping any liquid. Put it back in the freezer for 1 minute, then slide a finger through the butter; you should see a strip of clean saucer. If it isn't set, return the pot to the heat, stir constantly, and test again after 1 to 2 minutes.

To Sqirl away your butter, see pages 16–21.

Cranberry-apple butter Cranberries and Grapes

This is pure nostalgia. It's what I grew up drinking as juice, in jam form. Concord grape is the flavor everyone thinks of as grape jelly. We all grew up with it. But how can you do it in an adult way? Concord grape jam is the adult version. The skin is included in the jam because it makes for a nice texture and adds pectin.

Makes 6 to 8 half-pint jars

INGREDIENTS

3,200 g (7 lb)   **Concord grapes**
1,150 g (5¾ cups)   **sugar** (50% of the weight of grape pulp)
114 g (7½ Tbsp)   **lemon juice** (5% of the weight of grape pulp)

Prepare your plate test by putting a few saucers in the freezer.

Squeeze the grapes from their skins, using your fingers (it's easy to pop them out of the top where the stem connects to the grape). Put the skins in a large bowl and set aside. Put the fruit and any of its juice in a nonreactive pot.

Cook the fruit and juice over medium heat until soft, 3 to 5 minutes. Push the fruit and juice through a medium-mesh strainer and discard the seeds. Add the fruit and juice to the skins. This yields about 2,280 g grape pulp. Weigh yours so that you can add the correct amount of sugar (half of the weight of the grape pulp).

If you have more or less than 2,280 g grape pulp, you can figure out how much sugar and lemon juice you need by using the following formula:

Grams of grape pulp × 0.5 = grams of sugar
Grams of grape pulp × 0.05 = grams of lemon juice

Combine the sugar and lemon juice with the grape pulp. (You have the option to use the plumping technique here; see "Blending and Plumping" on page 14. Transfer the mixture to your jamming pot. Cook over medium-high heat, stirring frequently. As it gets closer to being done, you will start hearing a scraping or sizzling sound as you stir. It's ready when the jam appears thicker, glossy, and deep purple, and the temperature reaches 217°F (102°C), 13 to 18 minutes. When the jam nears this temperature, remove from the heat and perform a plate test.

Spoon a little of the jam onto a frozen saucer. Put the plate back in the freezer for 1 minute, then slide a finger through the jam. It's done when it parts and you see a strip of clean saucer. If it isn't set, return the pot to the heat, stir frequently, and test after another minute.

To Sqirl away your jam, see pages 16–21.

Concord grape jam Cranberries and Grapes

Concord grape jam Cranberries and Grapes

Concord grape jam Cranberries and Grapes

The scuppernong is very dear to me, reminiscent of the time I spent in Atlanta. Seeing one for the first time in Georgia—it was so bizarre; it was green and looked more like an olive than a grape. We had scuppernong jelly and scuppernong pie. They're among the few things you can't find anywhere but in the Deep South: scuppernongs, muscadines, and fresh peanuts (so delicious).

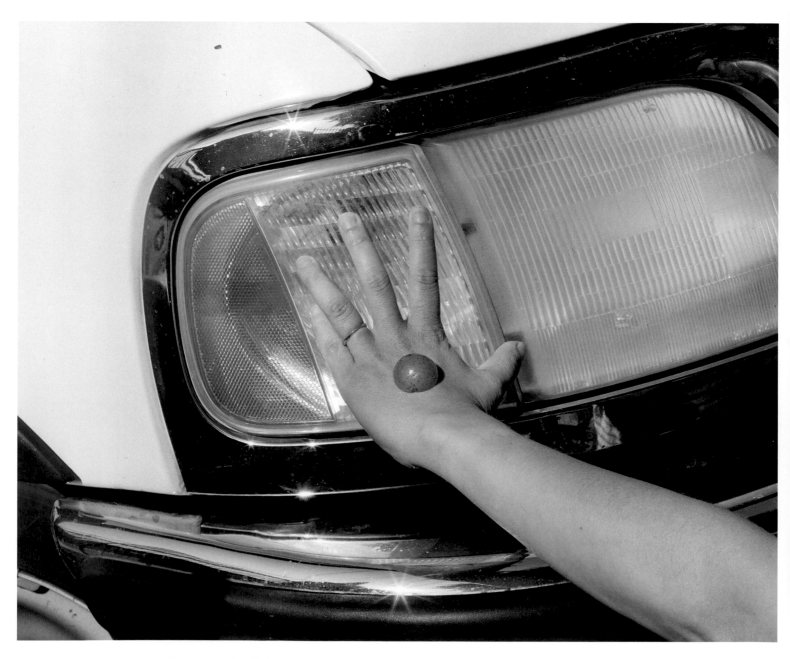

Scuppernong jam Cranberries and Grapes

Makes 6 to 8 half-pint jars

INGREDIENTS

3,290 g (7 lb 4 oz)   **scuppernong grapes**
1,050 g (5¼ cups)   **sugar** (50% of the weight of processed grapes)
105 g (7 Tbsp)   **lemon juice** (5% of the weight of processed grapes)

Use your fingers to squeeze the flesh of the grapes out of their skins (it's easy to pop them out of the top where the stem connects to the grape).

Put the skins in a bowl and set aside. Put the flesh and any of its juice in a medium pot. Cook the grape flesh and juice over medium heat until the grapes start to break down and soften, 10 to 15 minutes. Push them through a medium-mesh strainer set over a bowl and discard the seeds. If you're unable to push the pulp through the strainer, the grapes might not be cooked enough. Put them back on the stove and cook for 5 minutes.

Put the skins in a medium pot and add 3 cups water. Simmer over low heat until the skins have softened, about 20 minutes. Add more water if necessary to prevent the skins from burning. Stir occasionally. Discard the liquid and add the skins to the grape pulp. Transfer to a blender and blend until the skins break into small pieces. You should have about 2,048 g processed grapes.

If you have more or less than 2,048 g, you can figure out how much sugar and lemon juice you need by using the following formula:

Grams of processed grapes × 0.5 = grams of sugar
Grams of processed grapes × 0.05 = grams of lemon juice

(You have the option to use the plumping technique here; see "Blending and Plumping" on page 14.)

Combine the processed grapes, sugar, and lemon juice in your jamming pot. Cook over high heat, stirring frequently. It'll foam a lot and you'll know the jam is nearly done when the foam cooks off and you hear a sizzling sound as you stir. The jam is done when the jam is thick and glossy and the temperature reaches 217°F (102°C), 15 to 20 minutes. When the jam nears this temperature, remove from the heat and perform a plate test.

Spoon a little of the jam onto a frozen saucer. Put it back in the freezer for 1 minute, then slide a finger through the jam; you should see a strip of clean saucer. If it isn't set, return the pot to the heat, stir constantly, and test again after 1 to 2 minutes.

To Sqirl away your jam, see pages 16–21.

APPLES PEARS QUINCE PERSIMMONS & POMEGRANATES

170–209

Apples , Pears, Quince, Persimmons & Pomegranates

Save the Gravensteins[170] , Gravenstein apple butter[174] , Variation: Spiced Gravenstein apple butter[175] , Roasted honey apple butter[176] , Apple pectin[178] , Apple jelly[180] , Blackberry–apple butter[182] , Passion fruit–apple jelly[184] , Pomegranate–apple jelly[186] , Pomegranate persimmon butter[188] , Apple–lemon curd[190] , Honey cake with apple-lemon curd[192] , Warren pear butter[194] , Quince–raspberry butter[196] , Quince butter with rosemary[198] , Quince jelly[202] , Quince membrillo[204] , Fuyu persimmon butter[206] , Variation: Fuyu persimmon paste[207]

184

SAVE THE GRAVENSTEINS

Walker Apples, Graton, California

I'd tested a lot of varieties of apples for apple butter and wasn't perfectly happy with any of them . . . until the Gravenstein. Several years ago I read about these century-old apples growing outside of Sebastopol that are in danger of becoming extinct. They're crisp but tender and juicy, simultaneously sweet and tart, with a honeyed, floral, fruity aroma. And I knew I had to try them.

Come harvest, I called Walker Apples and let them know I wanted to buy some Gravensteins. The Walkers, who have grown apples for six generations, said to come up. So in the middle of September I got in my car and drove 437 miles from Los Angeles to Graton, California. I think they were surprised when I actually showed up and said, "Okay, I'm here for Gravensteins, let's fill my car up."

They weren't quite prepared for a random person to drive up and have her entire Prius filled with apples. I managed to fit fifteen cases—six hundred pounds—into the trunk, back seats, and front passenger side. I drove them home to Los Angeles with the bottom of the car very low to the ground and the interior a little bit steamy. And I made apple butter.

The thing about them that's so wonderful is their texture—they have some crunch, but they're also delicate. They don't have the fibrous toothiness of other apples. So when making apple butter, they become almost silky, without being overcooked or caramelized. So you really taste the flavor of the fruit.

Save the Gravensteins

I've made the same trip every year since. But now I fly up to Santa Rosa and rent a Jeep to drive them back down.

Once off the main highway, the road toward Walker Apples gets narrower and windier. You start to see apple trees all around. The Walker apple farm is one of the last standing examples of what Sebastapol used to be. Most of the Gravenstein orchards have given way to vineyards. You can't appreciate it more than by going up and seeing it firsthand.

To champion them is a relationship. They know me now. The joke is that I drive up and they laugh at me because the car is ridiculously full. Even if they don't care what I'm doing with the apples. A cook in the big city, making jam? Great. Does your check clear? See you next year.

Save the Gravensteins

Save the Gravensteins

GRAVENSTEIN APPLE BUTTER

There's no substitute for Gravenstein apples and their particular texture. But this recipe will work with any soft apples with good acidity.

Gravenstein apple butter Apples, Pears, Quince, Persimmons & Pomegranates

Braeburn apples, for example, which are a cross of Granny Smith with Lady Hamilton. Or Fuji apples. The spice mix lends itself to the holidays, the changing of the seasons. If you're feeling sentimental, add the spice in the variation. If you're honoring the fruit, keep it plain. Depending on the year and how sweet the apples are, we might adjust the amount of sugar to 50%. (We make a test batch and make a judgment call from there.)

Makes about 7 half-pint jars

INGREDIENTS

2,000 g (4 lb 6 oz)	**Gravenstein apples**
765 g (about 3¾ cups)	**sugar** (45% of the weight of apple puree)
34 g (2 Tbsp plus 1 tsp)	**lemon juice** (2% of the weight of apple puree)
½ tsp	**freshly grated nutmeg** (optional)

Prepare your plate test by putting a few saucers in the freezer.

Cut the apples into quarters and remove the cores. Put the apples in a large pot and cover with water. Bring the apples to a boil, then reduce the heat to a simmer. Simmer the apples, stirring once in a while so that they cook evenly, until fork tender, 35 to 40 minutes. Remove from the heat. Drain and discard the liquid.

Use a food mill to puree the apples (milling is faster while the fruit is still hot, but be careful, okay?). By using a food mill you will remove the peels and get great texture. You should have 1,700 g apple puree. If you have more or less, you can figure out how much sugar and lemon juice you need by using the following formula:

Grams of apple puree × 0.45 = grams of sugar
Grams of apple puree × 0.02 = grams of lemon juice

Combine the apple puree, sugar, and lemon juice in a jamming pot over high heat. Give it a good stir so that you don't get clumps of sugar. As the apple butter cooks, stir frequently, and when it's closer to setting, stir constantly to prevent scorching. Be careful, because apple butter will bubble not only vigorously but volcanically; lower the heat when necessary. Cook until the apple butter is thick and sludgy and reduced by nearly half, 35 to 40 minutes. (It's hard to read the temperature of fruit butters. You need to go by sight and testing.) Remove from the heat and add the nutmeg (if using). This is a good time for a plate test.

Spoon a little of the apple butter onto a frozen saucer. It should puff up (like a raised mole) when it hits the cold plate. Look at the edges; the butter should not be seeping any liquid. Put it back in the freezer for 1 minute, then slide a finger through the butter; you should see a strip of clean saucer. If it isn't set, return the pot to the heat, stir constantly, and test again after 1 to 2 minutes.

To Sqirl away your apple butter, see pages 16–21.

**Variation:
Spiced Gravenstein apple butter**

Put 6 bay leaves, 2 teaspoons whole cloves, 2 teaspoons whole black peppercorns, and 1 cinnamon stick in a small, dry pan over medium heat. Toast, stirring constantly, until fragrant, about 2 minutes. Crush the cinnamon stick. Put all of the spices in a sachet of cheesecloth tied with kitchen string. Add this to your jamming pot with the puree, sugar, and lemon juice. Toward the end of cooking the apple butter, remove your pot from the heat and use tongs to remove and discard the sachet of spices. This is a good time for your plate test.

Roasting the apples gives the apple butter a roasty flavor. If I had a smoker, I'd also try smoking the apples before pureeing them. (You could make a makeshift smoker in the oven . . .) This is a low-sugar apple butter, so not one to can. It isn't a jam we make at Sqirl but one that we would make if, let's say, we'd be using it quickly. As delicious with savory dishes as it is on top of pancakes.

Makes 4 half-pint jars

INGREDIENTS

For the apple puree

2,610 g (5 lb 12 oz)	**apples**
170 g (½ cup plus 2 Tbsp)	**honey**
60 g (¼ cup)	**lemon juice**
2	**fresh bay leaves**

For the apple butter

225 g (1¼ cups plus 2 Tbsp)	**sugar** (20% of the weight of apple puree)
30 g (2 Tbsp)	**lemon juice** (2% of the weight of apple puree)

Heat the oven to 400 F (205 C).

Prepare your plate test by putting a few saucers in the freezer.

Make the apple puree: Cut the apples into quarters, leaving the skin and core, and put them in a large roasting pan with 275 g (1 cup plus 2 Tbsp) water, the honey, lemon juice, and bay leaves. Cook until very soft, 45 minutes to 1 hour. Let cool slightly.

Discard the bay leaves and press the apples through a food mill to remove the cores, seeds, and peels (milling is faster while the fruit is still hot). You should have about 1,390 g apple puree. If you have more or less, you can figure out how much sugar and lemon juice you need by using the following formula:

Grams of apple puree × 0.20 = grams of sugar
Grams of apple puree × 0.02 = grams of lemon juice

Make the apple butter: Combine the apple puree, sugar, and lemon juice in a jamming pot over low heat. Stir occasionally at first and more often as the butter gets closer to being set. Cook until it's reduced by nearly half and very thick, way past applesauce—I'd call it sludgy—and much darker than applesauce, 30 to 45 minutes. (It's hard to read the temperature of fruit butters. You need to go by sight and testing.) Remove from the heat.

Perform a plate test: Spoon a little of the apple butter onto a frozen saucer. It should puff up (like a raised mole) when it hits the cold plate. Look at the edges; the butter should not be seeping any liquid. Put it back in the freezer for 1 minute, then slide a finger through the butter; you should see a strip of clean saucer. If it isn't set, return the pot to the heat, stir constantly, and test again after 1 to 2 minutes. Transfer to clean, lidded jars and store in the refrigerator for up to 1 month.

Roasted honey apple butter Apples, Pears, Quince, Persimmons & Pomegranates

APPLE PECTIN

To make jelly, you need pectin—the starch that when cooked at a high temperature with sugar and lemon juice forms a gel. For pectin, you have to boil the fruit in water, and the water needs to reduce enough so that you have a pectin that sets your gel with sugar and lemon. Knowing when the water has reduced enough: That's the trick. Look at the reduction; the water needs to reduce by about two-thirds. When rubbed between your fingers, the liquid should feel viscous and oily.

Makes about 2,000 g (8 cups)

INGREDIENTS

4,000 g (8 lb 12 oz) **Granny Smith apples**

Quarter the apples without peeling or coring them and set them aside. Put 4,000 g (17 cups) water in a large stockpot, cover, and bring to a boil. Add the apples. When the water returns to a boil, lower the heat to a simmer. Simmer until the liquid feels oily and viscous when rubbed between your fingers, 30 to 45 minutes.

Let cool slightly. Line a fine-mesh strainer with cheesecloth and strain the liquid into a large container; just let it sit, without pressing on the solids. It will take at least 30 minutes to fully drain. Discard the apples and store the liquid (pectin), covered, in the refrigerator for up to 1 week.

Apple Pectin Apples, Pears, Quince, Persimmons & Pomegranates

The best apples for apple jelly are crabapples. They make a nice firm jelly. But you can use any firm, crisp apple. Because jellies are sweet, they benefit from adding spices or other flavors. Tie a few sprigs of rosemary in a cheesecloth sachet and drop it in with the jelly as it cooks. Or try adding, toward the end of cooking, 1 teaspoon ground cardamom, the grated zest of 1 Meyer lemon, or several gratings of nutmeg using a rasp-style grater. Start checking for doneness with a plate test a few degrees before it reaches your final temperature to ensure a silky jelly. You don't want to cook it for so long that the jelly becomes chunky, with a caramelized sugar taste. The goal—to make a crystal-clear see-through jelly. It's a jam maker's way of showing off.

Note: Because jellies are sweet, they can benefit from herbs in cheesecloth or a little grated zest or nutmeg added at the end. Or for more flair, when canning, put a small sprig of rosemary or lavender, a bay leaf, a cinnamon stick, vanilla pod or a sliver of chile to the jar before pouring in the jelly.

Apple Jelly Apples , Pears, Quince, Persimmons & Pomegranates

Makes 8 or 9 half-pint jars

INGREDIENTS

1,900 g (7½ cups plus 1½ Tbsp)	**apple pectin** (page 178)
1,900 g (9½ cups)	**sugar** (100% of the weight of pectin)
150 g (¼ cup plus 2 Tbsp)	**lemon juice** (8% of the weight of pectin)

Prepare your plate test by putting a few saucers in the freezer.

Combine the apple pectin, sugar, and lemon juice in a jamming pot. Bring to a boil over high heat, stirring frequently. Using a spider or fine-mesh skimmer, skim the scum that rises to the top so that you have a clear final product. Dip the spider into a bowl of water and shake off the excess between skims to keep it clean. Boil for 30 minutes, continue to stir and skim, then reduce the heat to medium. Boil until the bubbles get smaller, the jelly looks a shade more golden, and the temperature nears 221°F (104°C), about an additional 10 minutes. Remove from the heat and perform a plate test.

Spoon a little of the jelly onto a frozen saucer. Put the plate back in the freezer for 1 minute, then slide a finger through the jelly. It's done when it parts and you see a strip of clean plate. If it isn't set, return the pot to the heat, stir frequently, and test again after 1 or 2 minutes.

To Sqirl away your jelly, see pages 16–21.

Apple Jelly Apples, Pears, Quince, Persimmons & Pomegranates

BLACKBERRY-APPLE BUTTER

I like to marry things when I feel they need marrying. There's something about adding blackberries here to balance the texture of the fibrous apple. (Also, I love apple-blackberry pie, so I wanted to try this as a jam.) Deseed the blackberries, using just the juice to enhance the color, texture, and amount of fruit sugar. You like the pop of acidity from the apple cider vinegar? I do, too.

Blackberry-apple butter Apples, Pears, Quince, Persimmons & Pomegranates

Makes 6 to 8 half-pint jars

INGREDIENTS

For the apple puree

1,146 g (3 lb 3 oz) **apples** (a soft variety such as Fuji)
45 g (3 Tbsp) **apple cider vinegar**

For the blackberry juice

908 g (2 lb) **blackberries**
850 g (4¼ cups) **sugar** (52% of the total weight of apple puree and blackberry juice)
68 g (¼ cup + 1½ tsp) **lemon juice** (4% of the total weight of apple puree and blackberry juice)

Prepare your plate test by putting a few saucers in the freezer.

Make the apple puree: Quarter the apples, leaving the core and skin. Put the apple quarters, 1,534 g (6½ cups) water, and the vinegar in a pot. Bring to a boil and then lower to a simmer, uncovered, and cook until soft, about 1 hour, stirring occasionally. Let cool slightly. Drain the apples, discarding the liquid.

Puree the apples in a food mill, which will remove the cores, skins, and seeds (milling is faster while the fruit is still hot). Set the puree aside. This makes about 1,116 g (4¾ cups) puree.

Make the blackberry juice: Put the blackberries and 3 Tbsp water in a small pot. Cook, uncovered, over low heat, stirring frequently, until the blackberries have released their juices and are soft, 20 to 30 minutes. Transfer the berries and liquid to a fine-mesh strainer (chinois) and press through until just the seeds are remaining. Discard the seeds. This makes about 531 g (2¼ cups) blackberry juice.

Add the blackberry juice to the apple puree. If you have more or less apple puree or blackberry juice (we use 68% apple puree to 32% blackberry juice), you can figure out how much sugar and lemon juice you need by using the following formula:

Grams of apple puree plus blackberry juice × 0.52 = grams of sugar
Grams of apple puree plus blackberry juice × 0.04 = grams of lemon juice

Combine the apple puree, blackberry juice, sugar, and lemon juice in a jamming pot over high heat. Cook, stirring frequently, until the butter has thickened and has small, vigorous bubbles, 15 to 20 minutes. It should come off your spatula as a single "sheet" of butter. Remove from the heat and perform a plate test.

Spoon a little of the apple butter onto a frozen saucer. Look at the edges; when done, the apple butter should not be seeping any liquid. Put the plate back in the freezer for 1 minute, then slide a finger through the apple butter. You should be able to see a strip of clean saucer. If it isn't set, return the pot to the heat, stir constantly, and test again after 1 to 2 minutes.

To Sqirl away your blackberry-apple butter, see pages 16–21.

Passion fruit and apple—it's fun confetti. There's something wonderful about getting the gel texture just right, and the sweetness of the apple married with the texture and acidity of the passion fruit makes this one exceptional preserve.

Passion fruit–apple jelly Apples , Pears, Quince, Persimmons & Pomegranates

Makes 6 to 8 half-pint jars

INGREDIENTS

1,020 g (2 lb 4 oz)	**passion fruit,** or more if needed
900 g (3¾ cups)	**apple pectin** (page 178)
1,500 g (7½ cups)	**sugar** (100% of the weight of apple pectin plus passion fruit pulp)
75 g (5 Tbsp)	**lemon juice** (5% of the weight of apple pectin plus passion fruit pulp)

Prepare your plate test by putting a few saucers in the freezer.

Cut the passion fruit in half crosswise. Scoop out the pulp with a spoon and put it in a bowl. Whisk vigorously with a fork until the pulp is broken up and quite loose. This is important: You'll use the seeds in the jelly. Use more passion fruit if you don't yield 600 g (2½ cups) of pulp.

Combine the passion fruit pulp, apple pectin, sugar, and lemon juice in a jamming pot. Bring to a boil over high heat. Using a spider or fine-mesh skimmer, start skimming scum that rises to the top to ensure a clear final product. Dip the spider into a bowl of water and shake off the excess to clean it between skims. Seeds might float to the top, so be careful not to skim out all the seeds.

Stirring constantly with a heat-resistant spatula to prevent scorching, boil until the bubbles get smaller, the jelly looks a shade deeper in color, and the temperature nears 221°F (105°C), indicating it's close to set, about 10 minutes. When the temperature nears 221°F, remove from the heat and perform a plate test (remember that it's better to run a plate test early rather than late).

Spoon a little of the jelly onto a frozen saucer. Put the plate back in the freezer for 1 minute, then slide a finger through the jelly. It's done when it parts and you see a strip of clean saucer. If it isn't set, return the pot to the heat, stir frequently, and test again after another minute.

To Sqirl away your jelly, see pages 16–21.

This jelly is just pretty. The pomegranate adds a surprising tartness as well as a festive pink color.

Note: The amount of juice in your pomegranates might vary. You'll need 413 g (1¾ cups) juice for this recipe. If you don't get enough, juice additional pomegranate fruit.

Makes 1,680 g, 6 to 8½ pints

INGREDIENTS

1,247g (2lb 12oz)	**pomegranate, or more as needed**
708g (3 cups)	**apple pectin** (page 178)
1,121g (about 5½ cups)	**sugar** (100% of the weight of pomegranate juice plus apple pectin)
68g (4 Tbsp plus 1½ tsp)	**lemon juice** (6% of the weight of pomegranate juice plus apple pectin)

Prepare your plate test by putting a few saucers in the freezer.

Fill a large bowl with cold water and set aside.

Cut off the blossom end of each pomegranate by cutting through and removing the crown at a slight angle. Score along the wider ribs of the pomegranates from the top to the stem end and crack open the pomegranates. Put segments of the pomegranates into the water and remove the fruit using your fingers. Remove as much of the white pith as possible. Drain and rinse the fruit in a strainer.

Put the fruit in a blender and pulse until the juice is released. Strain through a fine-mesh strainer and discard the seeds. You want 413 g (1¾ cups) pomegranate juice.

Combine the pomegranate juice, apple pectin, sugar, and lemon juice in a jamming pot. Bring to a boil over high heat. Using a spider, start skimming scum that rises to the top to ensure a clear final product. Dip the spider into a bowl of water to clean while skimming.

Stir constantly with a heatproof spatula to prevent scorching, until the bubbles become smaller and the jelly darker, indicating it's closer to setting. The jelly is set when the temperature reaches about 221°F (105°C), about 15 minutes. When the temperature nears 221°F, remove from the heat and perform a plate test.

Spoon a little of the jelly onto a frozen saucer. Put the plate back in the freezer for 1 minute, then slide a finger through the jelly. It's done when it parts and you see a strip of clean saucer. If it isn't set, return the pot to the heat, stir frequently, and test again after another 2 minutes.

To Sqirl away your jelly, see pages 16–21.

Pomegranate, like lemon juice, adds brightness to this persimmon butter. And it's great for color, so that what you end up with is a beautiful rosy butter.

If you get serious about making jam, find yourself a copper pot. The Mauviel 10.6-quart copper pan is perfect for home use.

Pomegranate-persimmon butter Apples, Pears, Quince, Persimmons & Pomegranates

Makes about 7 half-pint jars

Fuyu persimmon puree
1,816g (4 lb)   **Fuyu persimmons**
472g (3 Tbsp)   **water**
45g (3 Tbsp)   **lemon juice**
Pinch of citric acid (optional)

Pomegranate juice
1,247g (2lb 12oz)   **pomegranates**
60g (¼ cup)   **water**

413g (1¾ cups)   **pomegranate juice**
800g (4 cups)   **sugar** (45% of persimmon puree and pomegranate juice)
75g (5 Tbsp)   **lemon juice** (4% of persimmon puree and pomegranate juice)

Make the persimmon puree: Remove the calyx (the stem-end petal-like green part) from the persimmons, then peel and quarter the fruit. Put the persimmons in a medium pot with the water, lemon juice, and citric acid (if using). Cover with parchment paper cut to fit the diameter of the pot. Cook over medium heat until the persimmons are soft (the texture of a cooked sweet potato, tender enough to be pierced with a fork), about 30 minutes. Add water if necessary so that the persimmons don't scorch.

Drain the persimmons, discarding the water. Transfer the persimmons to a blender and puree until smooth. Weigh the pulp; you should have about 1,360 g (about 6 cups) puree.

Make the pomegranate juice: Fill a large bowl with cold water and set aside. Cut off the flower end of each pomegranate by cutting through and removing the crown at a slight angle. Score along the wider ribs of the pomegranates from the top to the stem end and crack open the pomegranates. Put the segments of pomegranates into the water and remove the fruit/seeds using your fingers. Remove as much of the white pith as possible. Drain the water and rinse the pomegranate fruit/seeds in a strainer.

Blend the pomegranate in a blender until juice is released. Strain through a fine-mesh strainer and discard the seeds. You want to yield 413 g (1¾ cups) of pomegranate juice.

If you have more or less persimmon puree or pomegranate juice (we use 76% persimmon puree to 24% pomegranate juice), you can figure out how much sugar and lemon juice you need by using the following formula:

$$\text{Grams of persimmon puree plus pomegranate juice} \times 0.45 = \text{grams of sugar}$$
$$\text{Grams of persimmon puree plus pomegranate juice} \times 0.04 = \text{grams of lemon juice}$$

Put the pomegranate juice, persimmon puree, sugar, and lemon juice in a jamming pot. Cook over high heat, stirring until set, about 20 to 25 minutes. It will start to make a sizzling sound on the bottom of the pot as you stir. The bubbles will get smaller and more vigorous as it gets closer to being set. The mixture should be homogeneous, and it should come off your spatula as a single "sheet" of butter. Remove from the heat and perform a plate test.

Spoon a little of the persimmon-pomegranate butter onto a frozen saucer. Look at the edges; when done, the butter should not be seeping any liquid. Put the plate back in the freezer for 1 minute, then slide a finger through the butter. You should be able to see a strip of clean saucer. If it isn't set, return the pot to the heat, stir constantly, and test again after 1 to 2 minutes.

To Sqirl away your pomegranate-persimmon butter, see pages 16–21.

Note: The amount of fruit in your pomegranates might vary. You'll need 413 g (1¾ cups) juice for this recipe. If you have less, juice additional pomegranate fruit.

This is a friendlier, sweeter lemon curd. If you want the taste of curd with a little less pucker, then this is the one for you. You're using the texture of the apple to make a slightly more delicate, not as acidic, but still really, really delicious lemon curd. I love citrus curd. Lemon curd. Key lime curd. I'd eat this with scones and clotted cream, too. Or in a layered sponge cake. I think I need help.

I use Belle de Boskoop apples for this curd—they have great acidity to balance their sweetness. Look for these at farmers' markets; you can also use a sweet-sharp variety such as McIntosh or Jonagold.

Makes 675 g (3 cups)

INGREDIENTS

454 g (1 lb)	apples
4	whole large eggs
3	egg yolks
300 g (1½ cups)	sugar
	Grated zest 2 lemons
120 g (½ cup)	lemon juice
126 g (9 Tbsp)	unsalted butter, cut into ¼-inch (6 mm) cubes
¼ tsp	salt

Quarter the apples and remove their stems and cores. Put the quartered apples in a large pot and add water to cover. Bring to a boil, then reduce to a simmer and cook, uncovered, until the apples are soft, 30 to 45 minutes.

Drain the apples, discarding the liquid, and transfer them to a blender. Blend until smooth. Push the apple puree through a medium-mesh strainer. You should have about 235 g (1 cup) apple puree.

Whisk together the whole eggs, egg yolks, and sugar in a large bowl until smooth. Add the apple puree, lemon zest, and lemon juice. Place the bowl over a pot of lightly simmering water (I like to do it low and slow, which takes a while but doesn't require any babysitting). Leave it on the water bath over low heat with the water just simmering. Cook until the mixture is thick like mayo and the temperature reaches 180°F (82°C), 40 to 50 minutes. Don't rush it or you will end up with eggy curd!

Remove the bowl from the heat. Whisk in the butter pieces a few at a time until incorporated. Whisk in the salt. For smooth curd, strain it through a chinois or fine-mesh strainer. Transfer to a container and place plastic wrap directly on top of the curd. Store, covered, in the refrigerator for up to 1 week.

Apple-lemon curd Apples, Pears, Quince, Persimmons & Pomegranates

Honey cake with apple-lemon curd Apples, Pears, Quince, Persimmons & Pomegranates

Apples and honey—as a snack that I refused to eat as a child, the nostalgia starts to click immediately. Of course it makes sense that I would want to do a cake version of it.

You can use whole-wheat pastry flour instead of the Grist & Toll. Just sift it before you measure it. To make a 1:1 simple syrup, put equal amounts of sugar and water (by weight) in a saucepan over medium heat. Stir until the sugar dissolves; remove from the heat and let cool.

Makes 1 (10-inch/25 cm) cake

INGREDIENTS

105 g (¾ cup plus 2 Tbsp)	**all-purpose flour**
52 g (¼ cup plus 3 Tbsp)	**soft wheat flour** (we use Grist & Toll Sonora)
42 g (3½ Tbsp)	**sugar**
¾ tsp	**salt**
1 tsp	**baking powder**
½ tsp	**baking soda**
⅛ tsp	**cream of tartar**
½ tsp	**ground cinnamon**
½ tsp	**ground cardamom**
⅛ tsp	**ground allspice**
1 large	**egg**
135 g (½ cup plus 1 Tbsp)	**orange juice**
	Finely grated zest of ½ orange
110 g (¼ cup)	**honey**
90 g (¼ cup plus 2 Tbsp)	**canola oil**
40 g (2 Tbsp)	**brewed coffee**
¾ tsp	**vanilla extract**
300 g (1¼ cups)	**simple syrup**
225 g (1 cup)	**apple-lemon curd** (page 190)
	Several dehydrated apple slices for garnish (optional)

Heat the oven to 325°F (165°C). Butter a 10-inch (25 cm) round cake pan and line it with parchment paper.

Put the flours, sugar, salt, baking powder, baking soda, cream of tartar, cinnamon, cardamom, and allspice in a large mixing bowl. Whisk to combine thoroughly. Set aside.

Put the egg, orange juice, orange zest, honey, oil, coffee, and vanilla in a large mixing bowl and mix thoroughly to emulsify.

Slow pour the egg mixture into the flour mixture and mix by hand. Make sure not to overmix.

Pour the batter into your prepared cake pan. Bake until a cake tester inserted in the center comes out clean, 45 minutes to 1 hour. Let cool completely.

Invert the cake and remove the parchment paper. With a serrated knife, trim the top of the cake just enough so that there is a mostly flat surface. Use a pastry brush to brush the simple syrup onto the cake.

Top the cake, using an offset spatula, with the apple-lemon curd so that it covers the entire top surface. Garnish with dehydrated apples (if using). Slice and serve immediately.

The issue I have with apples and pears is that they have a toothiness and texture that can't really be resolved. The Warren pear is the only pear that I've found silky enough to make an elegant butter. They're difficult to grow, so they're never sold commercially. We get them from Frog Hollow Farm. If you can't get Warren pears, know that there's no real substitution—but you can use a soft pear such as Bosc.

Liam Waldman with pears

Warren pear butter   Apples, Pears, Quince, Persimmons & Pomegranates

Makes 8 half-pint jars

INGREDIENTS

2,500 g (4 lb 6 oz)   **whole Warren pears**
972 g (4¾ cups plus 2 Tbsp)   **sugar** (45% of the weight of pear puree)
43 g (3 Tbsp)   **lemon juice** (2% of the weight of pear puree)
                                  1 vanilla pod, split and seeds scraped

Prepare your plate test by putting a few saucers in the freezer.

Cut the pears into quarters and remove the cores. Put the pears in a large pot and cover with water. Bring to a boil, then reduce the heat to a simmer. Simmer the pears, stirring once in a while so that they cook evenly, until fork tender, about 30 minutes. Remove from the heat. Drain and discard the liquid.

Use a food mill to puree the pears (milling is faster while the fruit is still hot). By using a food mill you will remove the peels and get great texture. You should have 2,160 g pear puree. If you have more or less, you can figure out how much sugar and lemon juice you need by using the following formula:

Grams of pear puree × 0.45 = grams of sugar
Grams of pear puree × 0.02 = grams of lemon juice

Combine the pear puree, sugar, and lemon juice in a jamming pot and place over high heat. Give it a good stir so that you don't get clumps of sugar. As the pear butter cooks, stir frequently, and when it's closer to setting, stir constantly to prevent scorching. Be careful, because the butter will bubble and splatter; lower the heat when necessary. Cook until the butter is thick and sludgy and reduced by nearly half, about 30 minutes. It should come off your spatula as a single "sheet" of butter. When done, the temperature should be about 208°F (98°C) (it's challenging to get a read). Remove from the heat.

Add the vanilla seeds by first smearing them along the side of the pot with your spatula. Then stir them into the jam until fully incorporated. This is a good time for a plate test.

Spoon a little of the pear butter onto a frozen saucer. It should puff up (like a raised mole) when it hits the cold plate. Look at the edges; the butter should not be seeping any liquid. Put it back in the freezer for 1 minute, then slide a finger through the butter; you should see a strip of clean saucer. If it isn't set, return the pot to the heat, stir constantly, and test again after 1 to 2 minutes.

To Sqirl away your butter, see pages 16–21.

QUINCE-RASPBERRY (*BRAINJAM*) BUTTER

Marrying quince with raspberry is the most elevated "butter" I could think of. We started this as a collaboration with the design collective Brain Dead. Quince had started coming into season, and it was also the end of raspberry season. It turned out to be a great transitional-season preserve, and one we'd never seen before. As in, "What even is that? It tastes amazing!" It's the fall surprise just like the rhubarb-kumquat jam is for spring.

Quince-raspberry butter Apples, Pears, Quince, Persimmons & Pomegranates

Makes 8 half-pint jars

INGREDIENTS

1,650 g (3 lb 10 oz)	**quince**
	1 lemon, cut in half
700 g (1 lb 9 oz)	**raspberries**
1,000 g (5 cups)	**sugar** (50% of the weight of quince puree plus raspberries)
80 g (5 Tbsp plus 1 tsp)	**lemon juice** (4% of the weight of quince puree plus raspberries)
176 g (⅔ cup)	**pectin** (yielded during the process) (10% of the weight of quince puree plus raspberries)

Prepare your plate test by putting a few saucers in the freezer.

Fill a large pot with 10 cups water and bring it to a boil.

Meanwhile, cut the quince into quarters. Remove the cores and set them aside (you'll use these later). Put the quartered quince in the boiling water. Squeeze the juice of 1 lemon into the water and drop in the rinds, too. Cook the quince, covered, over high heat until it's very soft and pink, 20 to 30 minutes. (It should definitely be pink; that's when it's ready.)

Remove the quince with a skimmer and set the pot of poaching liquid aside (do not discard).

Transfer the quince to a food mill and puree (milling is faster while the fruit is still hot). You should have 1,300 g quince puree (2,000 g of combined quince puree and raspberries). If you have more or less, you can make adjustments. We use 65% quince puree and 35% raspberries for this recipe. You can figure out how much sugar, lemon juice, and pectin you need by using the following formula:

Grams of quince puree plus raspberries × 0.50 = grams of sugar
Grams of quince puree plus raspberries × 0.04 = grams of lemon juice
Grams of quince puree plus raspberries × 0.10 = grams of pectin

Put the reserved cores and whatever's left in the food mill into the pot of poaching liquid over medium-high heat and boil for 30 minutes, stirring occasionally. The texture of the liquid should be like pectin, viscous and oily when rubbed between your fingers. Remove from the heat.

Line a fine-mesh strainer with cheesecloth and strain the liquid into a large container. Measure out 176 g (⅔ cup) of the pectin. Save the rest for another use (it's good pectin-y stuff) in a container in the freezer for up to 3 months.

Combine the quince puree, raspberries, pectin, sugar, and lemon juice in a jamming pot and place over high heat. Cook, stirring frequently with a heat-resistant spatula to prevent scorching, until the quince puree is very thick. It will bubble and spurt, so be careful; lower the heat when necessary. It's done when it's sludgy, has a nice pink hue, and is reduced by nearly half, about 40 minutes. It should come off your spatula as a single "sheet" of butter. Remove from the heat.

Perform a plate test by spooning a little of the quince-raspberry butter onto a frozen saucer. It should puff up (like a raised mole) when it hits the cold plate. Look at the edges; the butter should not be seeping any liquid. Put it back in the freezer for 1 minute, then slide a finger through the butter; you should see a strip of clean saucer. If it isn't set, return the pot to the heat, stir constantly, and test again after 1 to 2 minutes.

To Sqirl away your butter, see pages 16–21.

Kyle Ng of Braindead

Quince-raspberry butter Apples, Pears, Quince, Persimmons & Pomegranates

Here's the thing: I'm not a rosemary person when it comes to sweet stuff. But it feels like "'tis the season." So have this find its way onto a cheese plate or with a savory dish. You could serve it with a Sunday pork roast, for example.

Quince butter with rosemary Apples, Pears, Quince, Persimmons & Pomegranates

Makes 6 half-pint jars

INGREDIENTS

2,200 g (4 lb 6 oz)	**quince**
	1 lemon, cut in half
176 g (½ cup plus 3 Tbsp)	**pectin** (yielded during the process) (10% of the weight of quince puree)
792 g (about 4 cups)	**sugar** (45% of the weight of quince puree)
35 g (2 Tbsp plus 1 tsp)	**lemon juice** (2% of the weight of quince puree)
	1 sprig fresh rosemary

Prepare your plate test by putting a few saucers in the freezer.

Fill a large pot with 10 cups water and bring it to a boil.

Meanwhile, cut the quince into quarters. Remove the cores and set aside (you'll use these later). Put the quartered quince into the boiling water. Squeeze the juice of 1 lemon into the water and drop in the rinds, too. Cook the quince, covered, over high heat until it's very soft and pink, about 30 minutes. Remove from the heat.

Remove the quince with a skimmer and set the pot of poaching liquid aside (do not discard).

Transfer the quince to a food mill and puree (milling is faster while the fruit is still hot). You should have 1,760 g quince puree. If you have more or less, you can figure out how much sugar, lemon juice, and pectin you need by using the following formula:

Grams of quince puree × 0.45 = grams of sugar
Grams of quince puree × 0.02 = grams of lemon juice
Grams of quince puree × 0.10 = grams of pectin

Put the reserved cores and whatever solids are left in the food mill into the pot of poaching liquid over medium-high heat and boil for 30 minutes, stirring occasionally. The texture of the liquid should be viscous and oily when rubbed between your fingers. Remove from the heat.

Line a fine-mesh strainer with cheesecloth and strain the liquid into a large container. Measure out 176 g (⅔ cup) of the pectin. Use the rest for quince jelly (page 202); you can store it in a covered container in the refrigerator for up to 1 week and in the freezer for up to 3 months.

Combine the quince puree, pectin, sugar, and lemon juice in a jamming pot and place over high heat. Put the rosemary in a sachet of cheesecloth tied with kitchen string and add it to the pot. Cook, stirring frequently with a heat-resistant spatula to prevent scorching, until the quince puree is very thick. It will bubble and spurt, so be careful; lower the heat when necessary. It's done when it's sludgy, has a nice pink hue, and is reduced by nearly half, about 30 minutes. It should come off your spatula as a single "sheet" of butter. Toward the end of cooking, use tongs to remove and discard the rosemary. Remove from the heat.

Perform a plate test by spooning a little of the quince butter onto a frozen saucer. It should puff up (like a raised mole) when it hits the cold plate. Look at the edges; the butter should not be seeping any liquid. Put it back in the freezer for 1 minute, then slide a finger through the butter; you should see a strip of clean saucer. If it isn't set, return the pot to the heat, stir constantly, and test again after 1 to 2 minutes.

To Sqirl away your butter, see pages 16–21.

A quince-a-dence: I met Noah and Claire one morning walking down from the Sqirl studio to get coffee. The pair of siblings caught my eye, so I asked if they would pose for some photos in our cookbook. My fruit to photograph that day was quince, and by chance, Noah and Claire grew up with a quince tree in their backyard. —Scott

Quince at the Santa Monica Farmers Market Apples, Pears, Quince, Persimmons & Pomegranates

Noah Pellegrino Apples, Pears, Quince, Persimmons & Pomegranates

Quince jelly is what we make with leftover pectin from quince butter. We don't let anything go to waste.

Quince jelly Apples, Pears, Quince, Persimmons & Pomegranates

Makes 8 half-pint jars

INGREDIENTS

1,800 g (7 cups plus 3 Tbsp)	**quince pectin** (see page 198, Quince butter with rosemary)
1,800 g (9 cups)	**sugar** (100% of the weight of pectin)
90 g	**lemon juice** (5% of the weight of pectin)

Prepare your plate test by putting a few saucers in the freezer.

Combine the quince pectin, sugar, and lemon juice in a jamming pot. Bring to a boil over high heat, stirring frequently. Using a spider or fine-mesh skimmer, skim the scum that rises to the top so that you have a clear final product. Dip the spider into a bowl of water and shake off excess between skims to keep it clean. Boil for 25 minutes, continue to stir and skim, then reduce the heat to medium. Boil until the bubbles get smaller, the jelly looks a shade more golden, and the temperature nears 221°F (104°C), about 17 minutes more. Remove from the heat and perform a plate test.

Spoon a little of the jelly onto a frozen saucer. Put the plate back in the freezer for 1 minute, then slide a finger through the jelly. It's done when it parts and you see a strip of clean plate. If it isn't set, return the pot to the heat, stir frequently, and test again after 1 or 2 minutes.

To Sqirl away your jelly, see pages 16–21.

"Every year, our mom makes quince leather, quince paste (membrillo), and we take it home with us to different cities, college dorm fridges—eat some with cheese, some on toast, mix it in oatmeal. Sweet and mealy." –Noah & Claire

Quince jelly Apples, Pears, Quince, Persimmons & Pomegranates

QUINCE MEMBRILLO

The first time I had membrillo—thick jelly made from quince—was at Neal's Yard Dairy in London. So whenever I think of membrillo I remember the perfect blocks of it sitting among the cheeses at Neal's Yard.

Quince membrillo Apples, Pears, Quince, Persimmons & Pomegranates

Makes 1,134 g (2 lb 8 oz) quince membrillo

INGREDIENTS

	1 lemon, cut in half
1,045 g (5¼ cups)	**sugar** (100% of the weight of quince pulp)
30 g (2 Tbsp)	**lemon juice** (3% of the weight of quince pulp)

Fill a large bowl with cold water. Squeeze the juice of 1 lemon into the bowl of water and drop in the rinds, too.

Peel the quince and immediately put them into the lemon water to prevent them from browning.

Cut the quince into 1- to 2-inch (2.5 to 5 cm) chunks, including the cores, and return the cut fruit to the water. Once you're finished cutting the quince, drain the lemon water, discarding the lemon rinds, and put the quince in a large covered pot or Dutch oven. Add 1,180 g (5 cups) water.

Bring to a boil over high heat, then reduce to a simmer. Cook the quince until very soft and the liquid has reduced by about half, 1 to 1½ hours (leave the lid on for 45 minutes and then remove it so that the liquid can evaporate). You want to have about 472 g (2 cups) liquid remaining. Remove from the heat and let cool slightly.

Transfer the quince and liquid to a high-powered blender and blend until smooth. Push the blended quince through a medium-mesh strainer, using a ladle to help press it through. This is a time-consuming process. Work a little bit at a time, discarding seeds and tough pieces as you go. This yields about 1,045 g (4½ cups) strained quince pulp. But weigh your pulp so that you can add the same amount of sugar (by weight).

Line an 8-inch (20 cm) square cake pan with plastic wrap and set aside.

Transfer the pulp to a jamming pot. Add the sugar and bring to a boil, then immediately reduce the heat to a simmer. Cook over medium-low heat until very thick, stirring occasionally with a heatproof spatula, about 1½ hours. Stir more frequently as it thickens.

The mixture will become very thick with slow, large bubbles coming up from the bottom of the pot. The membrillo will be a deep red. When stirring, run a spatula across the bottom of the pot. If the gap is filled very slowly, the membrillo is ready. Immediately transfer the membrillo to the cake pan. Place plastic wrap directly on the surface of the quince paste. As it cools, it will continue to firm up. (If the membrillo doesn't set, you can transfer it back to the pot and keep cooking it down until it is the right consistency.)

Serve with your favorite cheeses. Or put it on a sandwich (see below). Store covered in plastic wrap at room temperature for up to 1 month.

Raclette and membrillo sandwich

Makes 2 sandwiches

INGREDIENTS

20 g (1½ Tbsp)	**unsalted butter**
	4 slices of bread from a crusty country loaf
142 g (5 oz)	**raclette cheese**, sliced
113 g (4 oz)	**quince membrillo** (page 204), sliced (you could use persimmon paste, too)

Heat the oven to 375°F (190°C).

Melt the butter in a skillet over low heat. Once melted, use a pastry brush to brush both sides of each slice of bread.

Toast the bread on both sides in a countertop toaster/toaster oven or in a skillet over medium heat until golden brown.

Put the bread slices on a work surface and top each slice of bread with about 36 g (1¼ oz) of the cheese. Put the bread on a baking sheet and bake until the cheese melts, about 2 minutes. Remove from the oven.

Put half of the membrillo on top of a slice of cheese-topped bread. Put the remaining membrillo on a second slice of cheese-topped bread. Top each membrillo-topped slice of bread with a cheese-topped slice of bread so that you have two sandwiches with membrillo in the center.

Transfer the sandwiches to a skillet over medium-high heat and put a weight on them—another heavy skillet or a flat plate or board with a couple of cans of beans on top. Cook until the underside is deep golden brown. Flip the sandwiches, weight them again, and cook until the other side is deep golden brown. Serve immediately.

Persimmon butter is similar to apple butter. Texture-wise it lends itself to being a delicious, soft schmear that can last through winter. You get such a good yield out of these things. If you have a tree with a lot of Fuyu persimmons, this is what you might want to do with them. The Fuyu persimmons should still be slightly firm—similar to the way you might want to eat an avocado—so that you can peel, quarter, and poach them.

Fuyu persimmon butter Apples, Pears, Quince, Persimmons & Pomegranates

Makes about 6 half-pint jars

INGREDIENTS

For the spice mix (optional)

3	**bay leaves**
2 tsp	**whole black peppercorns**
1 tsp	**whole cardamom seeds**
1	**cinnamon stick**

For the persimmon puree

2,100 g (4 lb 11 oz)	**Fuyu persimmons**
45 g (3 Tbsp)	**lemon juice**
	Pinch of citric acid (optional)
705 g (3½ cups)	**sugar** (45% of the weight of persimmon puree)
90 g (6 Tbsp)	**lemon juice** (6% of the weight of persimmon puree)
	Pinch of citric acid (optional)

Prepare your plate test by putting a few saucers in the freezer.

Make the spice mix, if using: Put the bay leaves, peppercorns, cardamom seeds, and cinnamon stick in a small, dry pan over medium heat. Toast, stirring constantly, until fragrant, about 2 minutes. Lightly crush the cinnamon stick. Put all of the spices in a cheesecloth sachet tied with kitchen string. Set aside.

Make the persimmon puree: Remove the calyx (the petal-like green part) from the persimmons, then peel and quarter the fruit. Put the persimmons in a medium pot with 590 g (2½ cups) water, the lemon juice, citric acid (if using), and the sachet of spices.

Cover with parchment paper cut to fit the diameter of the pot. Cook over medium heat until soft (the texture of a cooked sweet potato, easily pierced with a fork), about 30 minutes, adding more water if necessary so that the persimmons don't scorch. Drain the persimmons, discarding the water. Set aside the spice sack (you can reuse this while cooking the jam).

Transfer the persimmons to a blender and puree until smooth. Weigh the puree; you should have around 1,570 g. If you have more or less, you can figure out how much sugar and lemon juice you need by using the following formula:

Grams of persimmon puree × 0.45 = grams of sugar
Grams of persimmon puree × 0.06 = grams of lemon juice

Combine the persimmon puree, sugar, lemon juice, and citric acid (if using) in a jamming pot and add the sachet of spices. The butter splatters a lot as it cooks, so be sure to wear an apron and your gloves or kitchen mitts! Cook over high heat, stirring often, until the bubbles get smaller and more vigorous, 10 to 15 minutes. Remove and discard the spice sack at this point. When close to done, it will be shiny and will make a sizzling sound as you stir. It will come off your spatula as a single "sheet." Remove from the heat and perform a plate test.

Spoon a little of the persimmon butter onto a frozen saucer. It should puff up (like a raised mole) when it hits the cold plate. Look at the edges; the butter should not be seeping any liquid. Put it back in the freezer for 1 minute, then slide a finger through the butter; you should see a strip of clean saucer. If it isn't set, return the pot to the heat, stir constantly, and test again after 1 to 2 minutes.

To Sqirl away your butter, see pages 16–21.

Variation:
Fuyu persimmon paste

To make Fuyu persimmon paste, you just cook your persimmon butter lower and slower so that it thickens a lot more.

Line an 8-inch (20 cm) square pan with plastic wrap and set aside.

Combine the persimmon pulp with the sugar, lemon juice, citric acid (if using), and spice sachet in a jamming pot. Cook over medium-low heat, stirring occasionally, then more frequently as it thickens to prevent scorching. Because the mixture is over lower heat, it doesn't splatter much at all. The paste is going to thicken and set as most of the moisture evaporates (remove and discard the spice sack when it's close to done), after 50 to 70 minutes. You will know when it's done when you can cut through it with a spatula and clearly see the bottom of the pan.

Transfer the paste to the prepared pan. Press plastic wrap directly on top of the surface of the paste to prevent a skin from forming. It will continue to firm up as it cools.

This is a forgiving paste. If it doesn't set up, you can transfer it back to the pot and keep cooking. Store covered in plastic wrap at room temperature for up to 1 month.

Note: Citric acid, available at restaurant supply stores and online, helps keep the persimmons a bright orange color during cooking. Try it out; you might like the results.

Apples, Pears, Quince, Persimmons & Pomegranates

Apples, Pears, Quince, Persimmons & Pomegranates

CITRUS

212–255

Citrus

When Sqirl first opened we were getting all of our blood oranges from Rancho del Sol, an organic citrus farm east of San Diego, which grew three varieties. The deepest in color is the Moro blood orange, so that's what we used for the first marmalade ever sold at Sqirl.

Blood orange marmalade with vanilla bean Citrus

Makes 8 half-pint jars

INGREDIENTS

1,700 g (3 lb 12 oz)	**blood oranges**
1,300 g (6½ cups)	**sugar** (100% of the weight of blanched triangles)
1,040 g (4 cups plus 3 Tbsp)	**pectin** (yielded during the process) (80% of the weight of blanched triangles)
715 g (about 3 cups)	**blood orange juice** (from about 1,775 g [3 lb 4 oz] blood oranges—save the rinds!) (55% of the weight of blanched triangles)
135 g (7 Tbsp)	**lemon juice** (from 2 or 3 lemons—save these rinds, too) (10% of the weight of blanched triangles)
½	**vanilla pod, seeds scraped**

Day 1 Cut off the stem and blossom ends of the blood oranges. Cut the oranges into quarters lengthwise. Cut each quarter crosswise into thin (⅛-inch/3 mm) strips, creating triangles, removing any seeds as you go. Set aside the seeds and ends for the next day—you'll use these, along with any saved rinds from juicing, to make pectin for your marmalade.

Put the blood orange triangles in a container and cover with water. Cover the container and leave it out on the counter overnight.

Day 2 Prepare your plate test by putting a few saucers in the freezer.

Set a fine-mesh strainer over a stockpot and pour in the blood orange triangles and their liquid. Set aside the triangles. Measure the liquid and pour it into a large stockpot to make the pectin for your marmalade. Add enough water to the stockpot so that you have 14 cups total to make the pectin for your marmalade. Bring it to a boil over high heat.

Once the water is boiling, blanch the blood orange triangles in batches. Blanch for 5 minutes, then use a spider or fine-mesh skimmer to transfer the triangles to a strainer set over a bowl. Let the triangles drain for 10 minutes so that as much liquid as possible is collected. Add that liquid back to the pot.

Cut any rinds reserved from juicing (blood oranges and lemons) into finger-size pieces and add them to the pot too, along with the ends and seeds from the previous day.

Cook over high heat, stirring occasionally so that the bottom doesn't burn, until the liquid feels oily and viscous between your fingers, 30 to 35 minutes. Pour the liquid through a strainer set over a bowl. (We use a fine-mesh cone, and press the solids with a wooden dowel to squeeze as much pectin as we can. It creates a cloudy but strong pectin. We wouldn't recommend doing this if you're straining through a colander because too much stuff gets through.) You should have about 1,040 g pectin.

Meanwhile, weigh the blanched triangles. You should have 1,300 g. If you have more or less, you can figure out how much sugar, pectin, blood orange juice, and lemon juice you need by using the following formula:

Grams of blood orange triangles × 1.00 = grams of sugar
Grams of blood orange triangles × 0.80 = grams of pectin
Grams of blood orange triangles × 0.55 = grams of blood orange juice
Grams of blood orange triangles × 0.10 = grams of lemon juice

Heat the oven to 300°F (150°C). Pour the sugar into a baking dish and warm for 10 minutes.

Combine the warm sugar, blood orange triangles, pectin, blood orange juice, and lemon juice in a jamming pot over high heat. Stir—at first occasionally and then more frequently—with a heatproof spatula as your marmalade cooks. It initially will bubble gently. As it bubbles more vigorously it will start foaming (like foam on top of a soda just poured from a can). Skim off any scum or seeds with a spider or fine-mesh skimmer. Dip the spider into a large bowl of water and give it a shake to clean between skims. Cook until the bubbles get smaller, the marmalade looks a shade deeper in color, and the temperature nears 221°F (105°C), 25 to 30 minutes. A few degrees before the marmalade reaches this temperature, remove from the heat. Add the vanilla seeds to the side of the pot and then stir them into your marmalade. You can drop in the pod, too. This is a good time for a plate test.

Spoon a little of the marmalade gel onto a frozen saucer. Put the plate back in the freezer for 1 minute, then slide a finger through the marmalade. It's done when it parts and the jelly at the top of your finger furrows like a brow. You should then be able to remove your finger and see a strip of clean saucer. If it isn't set, return the pot to the heat, stir constantly, and test again after 1 to 2 minutes. Remove and discard the vanilla pod before you transfer your marmalade to jars.

To Sqirl away your marmalade, see pages 16–21.

Variation:
Blood orange marmalade with hibiscus

Add 20 g (½ cup) dried hibiscus to the stockpot of rinds when making the pectin. Make sure you push the hibiscus down into the water. Drain and discard the hibiscus along with the rinds. Omit the vanilla seeds.

The kitchen at Sqirl goes through a lot of fruit, which means we always have scraps around for making pectin. You might not. So if you need a lot of pectin, you can start from scratch with this recipe. Make the pectin with any oranges (blood oranges, Cara Cara, etc.). Use blood oranges for the blood orange jelly on page 216 or Seville oranges for the Seville orange jelly and marmalade on pages 226–29, for example.

Orange pectin Citrus

Makes 1,740 g (7½ cups)

INGREDIENTS

900 g (2 lb)   **oranges**

Day 1 Cut the citrus in half crosswise and juice. Save the juice for another use, such as for your jellies or marmalades.

Cut the rinds into finger-size pieces, put them in a pot, and cover them with 2,360 g (10 cups) water.

Cover the pot and bring to a boil over high heat. Reduce the heat to low and simmer until the liquid feels oily and viscous between your fingers, 45 minutes to 1 hour. It should feel like slightly slimy gel when rubbed between your fingers. Remove from the heat and let it sit out, covered, overnight.

Day 2 Line a fine-mesh strainer with cheesecloth and set it over a bowl. Strain the liquid from the pot, squeezing the citrus to release more liquid. Let the citrus sit for 30 minutes to fully drain, then discard the solids. Store the liquid pectin in the refrigerator until ready to use, up to 1 week. Or store it in a covered container in the freezer for up to 3 months.

You can put all of your citrus rinds into cheesecloth tied with kitchen string and drop that directly into your pot. When you remove it, make sure to squeeze out all of the liquid.

Orange pectin Citrus

Sqirl opened in March 2011—squarely in blood orange season.
So blood orange marmalade was the first thing we nailed. There was
so much juice and pectin from marmalade-ing that we were able
to make blood orange jelly, too.

Makes about 6 half-pint jars

INGREDIENTS

3	**lemons** (lemon juice is 6% of the weight of pectin)
1,300 g (6½ cups)	**sugar** (118% of the weight of pectin)
111 g (7 Tbsp)	**blood orange juice** (from making the pectin on page 214) (10% of the weight of pectin)
1,102 g (4½ cups)	**blood orange pectin** (page 214)
30 g (2 Tbsp)	**Campari** (3% of the weight of pectin)

Prepare your plate test by putting a few saucers in the freezer.

Juice the lemons, measure out 60 g (¼ cup) of the juice, and save the rest for another use. Put all the lemon halves in a sachet of cheesecloth tied with kitchen string. Set the juice and rinds aside.

Heat the oven to 300°F (105°C). Pour the sugar into a baking dish and warm for 10 minutes.

Combine the warm sugar, blood orange juice, lemon juice, cheesecloth sachet, and pectin in a jamming pot. Bring to a boil over high heat. Using a spider, start skimming scum that rises to the top to ensure a clear final product. Dip the spider into a bowl of water and shake off to clean between skims.

Stirring constantly with a heat-resistant spatula to prevent scorching, boil until the bubbles get smaller, the jelly looks a shade deeper in color, and the temperature nears 221°F (105°C), indicating it's close to set, about 10 minutes. When the jelly nears this temperature, remove from the heat and stir in the Campari. This is a good time for a plate test.

Spoon a little of the jelly onto a frozen saucer. Put the plate back in the freezer for 1 minute, then slide a finger through the jelly. It's done when it parts and the jelly at the top of your finger furrows like a brow. You should then be able to remove your finger and see a strip of clean saucer. If it isn't set, return the pot to the heat, stir constantly, and test again after 1 to 2 minutes.

To Sqirl away your jelly, see pages 16–21.

Blood orange jelly with Campari Citrus

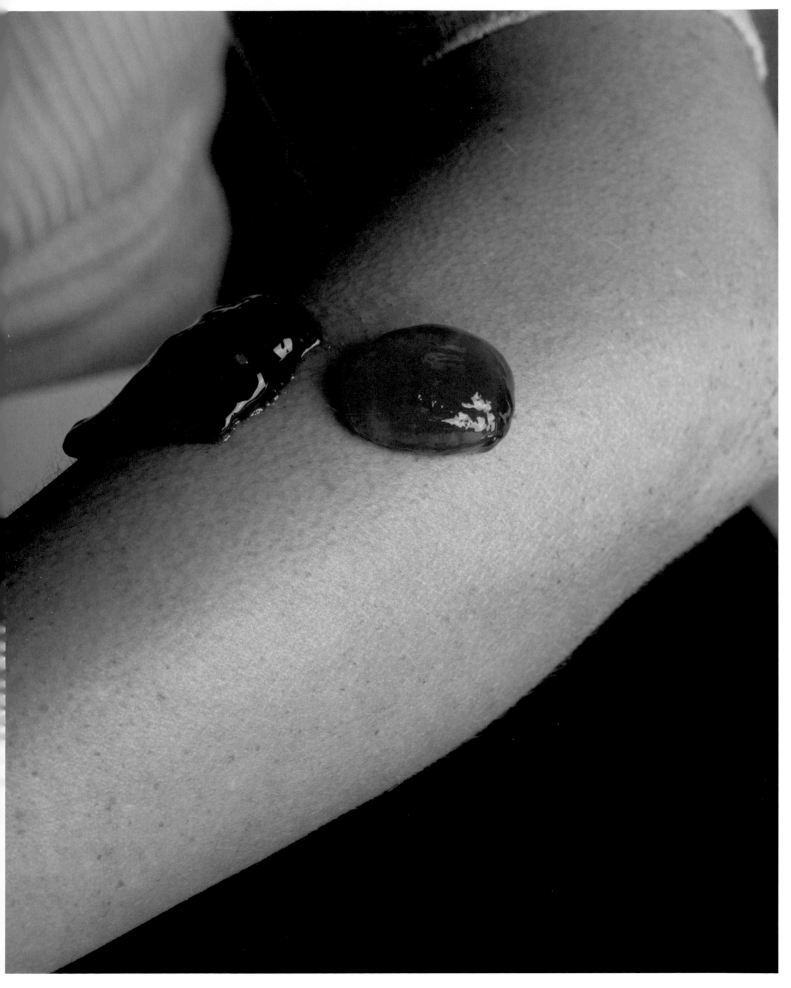

Blood orange jelly with Campari Citrus

CARA CARA ORANGE–MEYER LEMON–FENNEL MARMALADE

Our fennel fronds come from the neighborhood of Silverlake, where it's growing all over, just as citrus peaks. If you don't have access to fennel fronds, use toasted fennel seeds. The fronds are mild, so you also could use them along with toasted fennel seeds. If you don't like fennel at all, skip it. This is your world.

Makes about 6 half-pint jars

INGREDIENTS

1,030 g (2 lb 4 oz)	**Cara Cara oranges**
475 g (1 lb 1 oz)	**Meyer lemons**
25 g (¼ cup)	**roughly chopped fennel fronds, or 1 tsp toasted fennel seeds**
1,400 g (5½ cups)	**sugar** [122% of the weight of blanched citrus triangles]
800 g (3⅓ cups)	**Cara Cara orange juice** (from 2,200 g/4 lb 4 oz Cara Cara oranges) (70% of the weight of blanched citrus triangles)
150 g (½ cup plus 2 Tbsp)	**Meyer lemon juice** (from 500 g/1 lb 2 oz Meyer lemons) (13% of the weight of blanched citrus triangles)
1,000 g (4 cups)	**pectin** (yielded during the process) (87% of the weight of blanched citrus triangles)

Day 1 Cut off the stem and blossom ends of the oranges and lemons and set aside. Quarter the oranges and lemons lengthwise. Cut each quarter crosswise into thin (⅛-inch/3 mm) strips, creating triangles, removing any seeds as you go. Set aside the seeds and citrus ends for use the next day.

Put the orange and lemon triangles in a container and cover with water.

Cover the container and leave it out on the counter overnight.

Day 2 Prepare your plate test by putting a few saucers in the freezer.

Set a strainer over a bowl. Drain the triangles, reserving the liquid, and set them aside along with the cheesecloth sachet of fennel fronds.

Add enough water to the liquid so that you have 10 cups and pour it into a large pot or Dutch oven. Bring to a boil and blanch the triangles in batches for 30 seconds. Remove with a skimmer and transfer to a bowl.

You should have about 1,150 g blanched citrus triangles. If you have more or less, you can figure out how much sugar, Cara Cara juice, Meyer lemon juice, and pectin you will need by using the following formula:

Grams of blanched citrus triangles × 1.22 = grams of sugar
Grams of blanched citrus triangles × 0.70 = grams of Cara Cara juice
Grams of blanched citrus triangles × 0.13 = grams of Meyer lemon juice
Grams of blanched citrus triangles × 0.87 = grams of pectin

Put the reserved seeds and citrus ends in the blanching liquid. Cook over high heat until the liquid is viscous and oily when rubbed between your fingers, about 30 minutes. Remove from the heat. Line a fine-mesh strainer with cheesecloth and set it over a bowl. Strain the liquid. Let the the ends, seeds, and peels drain for 10 to 15 minutes to extract as much liquid as possible. Discard the ends, seeds, and peels. You should have 1,000 g liquid pectin.

Heat the oven to 300°F (150°C). Pour the sugar into a baking dish and warm for 10 minutes.

Combine the warm sugar, orange and lemon triangles, orange juice, Meyer lemon juice, and pectin in a jamming pot over high heat. Put the fennel fronds in a cheesecloth sachet tied with kitchen string and drop it in. Stir constantly with a heat-resistant spatula as it cooks. At first, it will bubble gently. Once it starts bubbling more vigorously, it will start to foam. Keep a close eye and continue to stir as needed to prevent the bottom from scorching. Cook until the bubbles get smaller, the marmalade is a shade deeper in color, and the temperature nears 221°F (105°C), about 45 minutes.

When the marmalade nears the point of setting (a few degrees before 221°F), remove the pot from the heat. Remove the cheesecloth sachet with tongs, squeezing the bag over the pot to extract any liquid. Give your jam a stir and discard the sachet. This is a good time for a plate test.

Spoon a little of the marmalade gel onto a frozen saucer. Put the plate back in the freezer for 1 minute, then slide a finger through the marmalade. It's done when it parts, you see a strip of clean saucer, and the jelly at the top of your finger furrows like a brow. If it isn't set, return the pot to the heat, stir constantly, and test again after 1 to 2 minutes.

To Sqirl away your jelly, see pages 16–21.

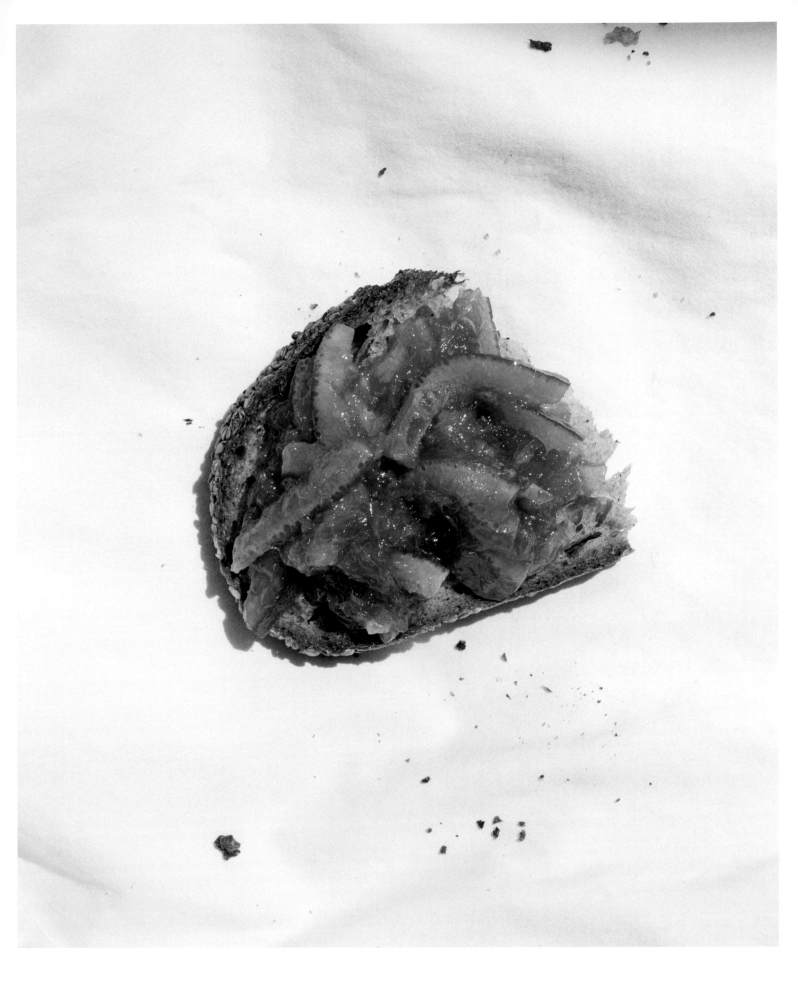

Cara Cara orange–Meyer lemon–fennel marmalade Citrus

This version of Cara Cara orange marmalade gets a little bit of grapefruit juice to create, along with tart hibiscus, a different flavor profile. It's one of my favorite marmalades. Of course we save any rinds for pectin—except for grapefruit rinds, because they will make the pectin too bitter (they are better candied; see page 248). Just use the grapefruit juice here.

Cara Cara orange marmalade with hibiscus Citrus

Makes 8 half-pint jars

INGREDIENTS

1,700 g (3 lb 12 oz)	**Cara Cara oranges**
1,300 g (6½ cups)	**sugar** (100% of the weight of blanched citrus triangles)
1,040 g (4 cups plus 2½ Tbsp)	**pectin (yielded during the process)** (80% of the weight of blanched citrus triangles)
357 g (1½ cups)	**Cara Cara orange juice** (from about 885 g/about 2 lb Cara Cara oranges—save the rinds!) (27% of the weight of blanched citrus triangles)
357 g (1½ cups)	**grapefruit juice** (from about 565 g/1 lb 4 oz grapefruit) (27% of the weight of blanched triangles)
135 g (½ cup plus 1 Tbsp)	**lemon juice** (from 2 or 3 lemons—yep, save the rinds) (10% of the weight of blanched citrus triangles)
20 g (½ cup)	**dried hibiscus**

Day 1 Cut off the stem and blossom ends of the oranges. Cut the oranges into quarters lengthwise. Cut each quarter crosswise into thin (⅛-inch/3 mm) strips, creating triangles, removing any seeds as you go. Set aside the seeds and ends for the next day—you'll use these, along with any saved rinds from juicing, to make pectin for your marmalade.

Put the orange triangles in a container and cover with water. Cover the container and leave it out on the counter overnight.

Day 2 Prepare your plate test by putting a few saucers in the freezer.

Set a fine-mesh strainer over a large stockpot and pour in the orange triangles and their liquid. Set aside the triangles. Measure the liquid and pour it back into the pot to make the pectin for your marmalade. Add enough water to the stockpot so that you have 14 cups total. Bring it to a boil over high heat.

Once the water is boiling, blanch the orange triangles in batches. Blanch for 5 minutes, then use a spider or fine-mesh skimmer to transfer the triangles to a strainer set over a bowl. Let the triangles drain for 10 minutes so that as much liquid as possible is collected. Add that liquid back to the pot.

Cut any rinds reserved from juicing (oranges and lemons) into finger-size pieces and add them to the pot too, along with the ends and seeds from the previous day.

Cook over high heat, stirring occasionally so that the bottom doesn't burn, until the liquid feels oily and viscous between your fingers, 30 to 35 minutes. Pour the liquid through a strainer set over a bowl. (We use a fine-mesh cone, and press the solids with a wooden dowel to squeeze as much pectin as we can. It creates a cloudy but strong pectin. We wouldn't recommend doing this if you're straining through a colander because too much stuff gets through.) You should have about 1,100 g liquid pectin.

Meanwhile, weigh the blanched triangles. You should have 1,300 g. If you have more or less, you can figure out how much sugar, pectin, orange juice, grapefruit juice, and lemon juice you need by using the following formula:

Heat the oven to 300°F (150°C). Pour the sugar into a baking dish and warm for 10 minutes.

Combine the warm sugar, orange triangles, pectin, orange juice, grapefruit juice, and lemon juice in a jamming pot over high heat. Put the hibiscus in a sachet of cheesecloth tied with kitchen string and drop that in. Stir—at first occasionally and then more frequently—with a heatproof spatula as your marmalade cooks. It initially will bubble gently. As it bubbles more vigorously it will start foaming (like foam on top of a soda just poured from a can). Skim off any scum or seeds with a spider or fine-mesh skimmer. Dip the spider into a large bowl of water and give it a shake to clean between skims. Cook until the bubbles get smaller, the marmalade looks a shade deeper in color, and the temperature nears 218°F (103°C), about 50 minutes. A few degrees before the marmalade reaches this temperature, remove from the heat. Remove the cheesecloth sachet with tongs, squeezing the bag over the pot to extract any liquid. Discard the sachet. This is a good time for a plate test.

Spoon a little of the marmalade gel onto a frozen saucer. Put the plate back in the freezer for 1 minute, then slide a finger through the marmalade. It's done when it parts and the jelly at the top of your finger furrows like a brow. You should then be able to remove your finger and see a strip of clean saucer. If it isn't set, return the pot to the heat, stir constantly, and test again after 1 to 2 minutes.

To Sqirl away your marmalade, see pages 16–21.

Grams of blanched blood orange triangles × 1.00 = grams of sugar
Grams of blanched blood orange triangles × 0.80 = grams of pectin
Grams of blanched blood orange triangles × 0.27 = grams of orange juice
Grams of blanched orange triangles × 0.27 = grams of grapefruit juice
Grams of blanched blood orange triangles × 0.10 = grams of lemon juice

Cara Cara orange marmalade with hibiscus Citrus

Cara Cara orange marmalade with hibiscus Citrus

THE SEVILLE ORANGES OF STUDIO CITY

Every year, around the end of January or beginning of February, John Mattingly calls to say that his Seville oranges are ripe and ready to be picked. "It is time and you have to take them all."

John, who's British, moved to his current home in Studio City in 1979 and a few years later ordered a Seville orange tree from Florida through Sperling Nursery in Calabasas. That was when Joe Sperling (R.I.P.) would help you track down hard-to-find plants just so you could make marmalade.

The Seville orange tree isn't indigenous to California. But John knew exactly what he was looking for. The way he tells it, the Seville orange tree came from China "way back" and ended up on ships to Spain. In the late eighteenth century a boatload of these oranges was shipwrecked in Dundee, Scotland. "A woman there, she must have been in the business, I suppose, bought the whole lot and started the orange marmalade industry, single-handedly."

John's tree came in a five-gallon pot and took five years to bear its first fruit. Two decades later Sqirl gets at least eighty pounds a season (sometimes double or triple that), and John keeps ten to twenty pounds for himself.

"There was a French bakery down around the corner who used to take them," John says, "but they left the country. I've always given them away to people who know what they are. I gave them to a pub once. One year I took them all to my church and said these are not for eating, don't take them if you aren't going to make marmalade. They found out the hard way."

A Seville orange is a sour orange. The peel is bitter, and the pulp is sour and not to be eaten as a fresh fruit. But it makes for great preserves because of its strong flavor and high pectin content, which is what gives marmalade its set.

Because you're using the whole fruit, peel and all, the oranges shouldn't be sprayed. (John has never, ever sprayed his tree.) The sooner you use them, the better, because the pectin starts to diminish as soon as the fruit is picked.

The day I get the call from John, I drive to Studio City and together we pick the Sevilles. It's usually just the two of us. I took David once, but he was afraid of the golden retriever. The golden retriever just wanted pets!

John and I have a system. I climb up a ladder with a fruit picker—a long pole with an attached basket—and huck the oranges into the backyard pool. From there he collects them with a pool net. Job done.

The Seville Oranges of Studio City

SEVILLE ORANGE JELLY

You can use the reserved Seville orange juice from making Seville orange pectin.

Seville orange jelly Citrus

Makes about 6 half-pint jars

INGREDIENTS

60 g (¼ cup)	**lemon juice** (from 3 lemons) (lemon juice is 118% of the weight of pectin)
1,300 g (6½ cups)	**sugar** (118% of the weight of pectin)
1,062 g (4½ cups)	**Seville orange pectin** (page 214)
11 g (7 Tbsp)	**Seville orange juice** (10% of the weight of pectin)

Prepare your plate test by putting a few saucers in the freezer.

Juice the lemons, measure out 60 g (¼ cup) juice, and save the rest for another use. Put all the lemon rinds in a sachet of cheesecloth tied with kitchen string and set aside.

Heat the oven to 300°F (150°C). Pour the sugar into a baking dish and warm in the oven for 10 minutes.

Combine the warm sugar, pectin, Seville orange juice, cheesecloth sachet, and lemon juice in a jamming pot and bring to a boil over high heat. Stir frequently with a heat-resistant spatula as it cooks to prevent scorching. Using a spider, start skimming scum that rises to the top to ensure a clear final product. Dip the spider into a bowl of water and give it a shake to clean between skims.

Cook until the bubbles get smaller, the jelly is a shade deeper in color, and the temperature reaches 221°F (105°C), 10 to 15 minutes. When the jelly nears the point of setting (a few degrees before 221°F), remove from the heat. Remove the cheesecloth sachet with tongs, squeezing the bag over the pot to extract any liquid. Discard the sachet. This is a good time for a plate test.

Spoon a little of the jelly onto a frozen saucer. Put the plate back in the freezer for 1 minute, then slide a finger through the marmalade. It's done when it parts and you see a strip of clean saucer. If it isn't set, return the pot to the heat, stir constantly, and test again after 1 to 2 minutes.

To Sqirl away your jelly, see pages 16–21.

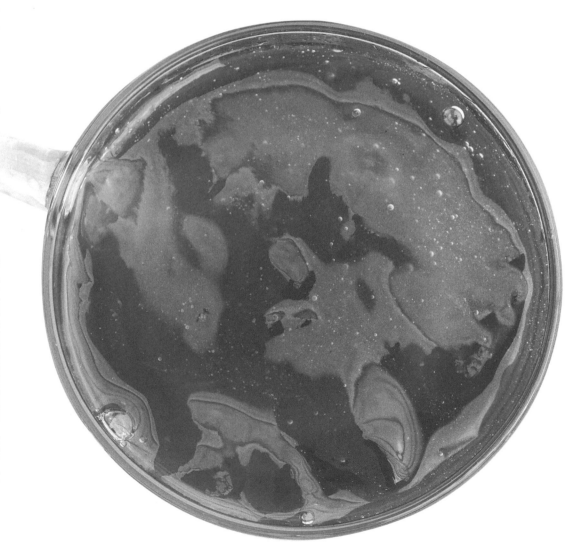

Seville orange jelly Citrus

This is what's called a shred, because the peel is sliced into fine "shreds" or slices. We make this marmalade in the style of Vivien Lloyd, whose preserves are known for sweeping awards at contests of all kinds (the Marmalade Awards, Fortnum & Mason's Chutney Challenge, and so on) in her native England and internationally. Her marmalade method calls for removing the fruit and pulp of fresh Seville oranges, then cutting and boiling the peel, rather than boiling the citrus whole first. The champion knows best.

Seville orange marmalade Citrus

Makes 6 or 7 half-pint jars

INGREDIENTS

680 g (1 lb 8 oz) **Seville oranges** (Seville orange juice is 16% of the weight of whole oranges plus lemon)
250 g (about 9 oz) **lemons** (lemon juice is 9% of the weight of whole oranges plus lemons)
1,400 g (7 cups) **sugar** (151% of the weight of whole oranges plus lemon)

Day 1 Cut the Seville oranges and lemons in half crosswise and juice, being careful to maintain the shape of the fruit halves. Set the rinds aside. You should have about 145 g (about ½ cup plus 2 Tbsp) orange juice and about 85 g (¼ cup plus 1 Tbsp) lemon juice. Combine the juices and set aside. Collect the seeds and set aside.

Using a spoon or your fingers, scoop out the membranes and pulp from the oranges and lemon, setting aside the peels. Put the membranes and pulp in a food processor and pulse until the membranes are finely chopped.

Put the pulp mixture and the reserved seeds in a sachet of cheesecloth tied with kitchen string. Put the sachet in a 4-quart (4 L) container and set aside.

Quarter the peels by cutting the halves lengthwise. Slice the quarters (you can stack a few at a time) lengthwise into very thin (2 mm) strips.

Put the juices and sliced peels in the container with the cheesecloth sachet. Add 1,770 g (7½ cups) water, cover, and leave it out on the counter overnight.

Day 2 Prepare your plate test by putting a few saucers in the freezer.

Put the contents of the container in a jamming pot and bring to a boil, then reduce to a simmer. Cook gently until the peels are soft, about 2 hours. The total volume of peels and liquid should be about 1 quart (1 L).

Heat the oven to 300°F (150°C). Pour the sugar into a baking dish and warm in the oven for 10 minutes.

Add the warm sugar to the jamming pot and stir until dissolved.

Cook the marmalade over high heat, stirring as needed with a heat-resistant spatula to prevent scorching. Skim off any scum by using a spider or fine-mesh skimmer. Dip the spider into a bowl of water between skims to keep it clean. As the marmalade gets closer to setting, it will foam a lot. Cook until the bubbles get smaller, the marmalade is glossy, and the temperature nears 221°F (105°C), 20 to 25 minutes. When the marmalade is close to the setting point (a few degrees before 221°F), remove from the heat. Remove the cheesecloth sachet with tongs, squeezing the bag over the pot to extract any liquid. Discard the sachet. This is a good time for a plate test.

Spoon a little of the marmalade gel onto a frozen saucer. Put the plate back in the freezer for 1 minute, then slide a finger through the marmalade. It's done when it parts and the marmalade at the top of your finger furrows like a brow. You should be able to see a strip of clean saucer. If it isn't set, return to the heat, stir constantly, and test again after 1 to 2 minutes.

To Sqirl away your marmalade, see pages 16–21.

The inspiration behind this marmalade was Earl Grey, known for its floral bergamot aroma and flavor. But in the place of black tea we used roasted buckwheat for its tea-like nutty flavor without the caffeine.

Bergamot-buckwheat marmalade Citrus

Makes 8 half-pint jars

INGREDIENTS

1,550 g (3 lb 7 oz)	**bergamots**
1,320 g (6½ cups plus 1½ Tbsp)	**sugar** (120% of the weight of blanched bergamot triangles)
50 g (3 Tbsp plus 1 tsp)	**lemon juice** (4.5% of the weight of blanched bergamot triangles)
3,075 g (13 cups)	**water** (280% of the weight of blanched bergamot triangles)
18 g	**roasted buckwheat grains** (1.2% of the weight of blanched bergamot triangles)

Prepare your plate test by putting a few saucers in the freezer.

Cut off the stem and blossom ends of the bergamots. Cut the bergamots into quarters lengthwise. Cut each quarter crosswise into thin (⅛-inch/3 mm) strips, creating triangles, removing any seeds as you go. Put the seeds and ends into a sachet of cheesecloth tied with kitchen string and set aside.

Fill a large pot with water and bring it to a boil. Add the bergamot triangles and cover. Bring it back to a boil, then reduce the heat to a simmer and cook for 3 minutes. Drain, discarding the liquid. Repeat this process one more time. (This helps mitigate the bitterness of the bergamot, but I've noted that others—such as pastry chef and author David Lebovitz—blanch the bergamot just once. Maybe this works, but I have yet to try it.)

Weigh your triangles. You should have 1,100 g blanched triangles. If you have more or less, you can figure out how much sugar, lemon juice, water, and buckwheat you need with the following formula:

Grams of blanched bergamot triangles × 1.20 = grams of sugar
Grams of blanched bergamot triangles × 0.045 = grams of lemon juice
Grams of blanched bergamot triangles × 2.80 = grams of water

Heat the oven to 300°F (150°C). Pour the sugar into a baking dish and warm for 10 minutes.

Put the triangles back into your pot along with the cheesecloth sachet of seeds and ends. Cover with 13 cups water. Put the buckwheat grains in a tea bag or cheesecloth sachet tied with kitchen string and add it to the pot. Bring to a boil.

Add the warmed sugar and bring back to a boil, about 10 minutes, stirring and scraping the bottom of the pot with a heatproof spatula so that the sugar doesn't caramelize or burn. It initially will bubble gently. As it bubbles more vigorously it will start foaming. Skim off any scum or seeds with a spider or fine-mesh skimmer. Dip the spider into a large bowl of water and give it a shake to clean between skims.

Cook, still stirring, until the bubbles get smaller, the marmalade looks a shade deeper in color, and the temperature nears 217°F (102°C), about 50 minutes. A few degrees before the marmalade reaches this temperature, remove from the heat. Remove the cheesecloth sachet of seeds and ends and the sachet of buckwheat with tongs, squeezing the bags over the pot to extract any liquid. Discard the sachets. Give your jam a stir. This is a good time for a plate test.

Spoon a little of the marmalade gel onto a frozen saucer. Put the plate back in the freezer for 1 minute, then slide a finger through the marmalade. It's done when it parts and the jelly at the top of your finger furrows like a brow. You should then be able to remove your finger and see a strip of clean saucer. If it isn't set, return the pot to the heat, stir constantly, and test again after 1 to 2 minutes.

To Sqirl away your marmalade, see pages 16–21.

LEMON-LIME SHRED

Sqirl's take on the very British lemon marmalade Robertson's Silver Shred is this lemon-lime version. "Shred" refers to the thin slices of peel. This is a great example of how we make marmalades, with a clear lemon and lime taste. Ahh, Sprite in jam form.

Lemon-lime shred Citrus

Makes about 8 half-pint jars

INGREDIENTS

500 g (1 lb 2 oz)　　**lemons** (lemon juice is 18% of the weight of whole lemons plus limes)
500 g (1 lb 2 oz)　　**limes** (lime juice is 22% of the weight of whole lemons plus limes)
1,500 g (7½ cups)　**sugar** (150% of the weight of whole lemons plus limes)

Day 1 Cut the lemons and limes in half crosswise. Juice the lemons and limes (have a few extra on hand in case you need more juice), being careful to maintain the shape of the fruit halves. Set the rinds aside. You should have about 180 g (¾ cup) lemon juice and 225 g (¾ cup plus 3 Tbsp) lime juice; pour the juices and 2,596 g (11 cups) water into a 4-quart (4 L) container and set aside.

Cut the leftover lemon and lime halves in half lengthwise so that you now have quartered peels. Scrape out the membranes, pulp, and seeds and transfer a bowl; you can do this with a spoon or by pulling with your fingers or using a sharp paring knife. You don't want a whole lot of white pith left on the peel. Set the peels aside for now.

Transfer the membrane, pulp, and seeds to the bowl of a food processor and pulse until the membranes are finely chopped. Transfer to a cheesecloth sachet tied with kitchen string and place in the container with the water and juice.

Slice the lemon and lime peels (you can stack a few at a time) lengthwise into very thin (2 mm) strips. Add the peels to the container with the juice, water, and cheesecloth sachet. Cover and leave out on the counter overnight.

Day 2 Prepare your plate test by putting a few saucers in the freezer.

Pour all of the contents of the container into a jamming pot. Bring to a boil, then reduce to a simmer. Simmer gently for about 2 hours, until the peels are very tender and the volume is reduced to about one-third. You should have about 1½ quarts (1.5 L) peels and liquid.

Heat the oven to 300°F (150°C). Pour the sugar into a baking dish and warm in the oven for 10 minutes.

Add the warm sugar to the jamming pot and stir gently to help it dissolve. Continue to cook over high heat, stirring with a heat-resistant spatula to prevent scorching. At first, the mixture will bubble gently. As it bubbles more vigorously it will start foaming. Skim off any scum with a spider or fine-mesh skimmer. Dip the spider into a bowl of water between skims to keep it clean. Watch the marmalade closely and continue to stir. Cook until the bubbles get smaller, the marmalade darkens a shade in color, and the temperature nears 221°F (105°C), about 15 minutes. When the marmalade nears the point of setting (a few degrees before 221°F), remove from the heat. Remove the cheesecloth sachet with tongs, squeezing the bag over the pot to extract any liquid. Discard the sachet and give the jam a stir. This is a good time for a plate test.

Spoon a little of the marmalade gel onto a frozen saucer. Put the plate back in the freezer for 1 minute, then slide a finger through the marmalade. It's done when it parts and the marmalade at the top of your finger furrows like a brow. You should then be able to remove your finger and see a strip of clean saucer. If it isn't set, return the pot to the heat, stir constantly, and test again after 1 to 2 minutes.

To Sqirl away your marmalade, see pages 16–21.

Variation: Lemon-lime shred with makrut lime

On day 2, put 10 makrut lime leaves into a cheesecloth sachet and crush with a rolling pin or wooden spoon or your hands to release the leaves' essence. Add it to the jamming pot along with the other ingredients to be boiled down. Add the grated zest of 2 makrut limes when you add the warmed sugar. Proceed with the rest of the recipe above, removing the lime leaf sachet when you remove the sachet with the citrus trimmings.

Citrus

Citrus

Making a kumquat jam is almost like sitting and reading Moby-Dick. You're in it for the long haul. You slice off all the ends, take out the seeds, and cut what remains into circles ⅛ inch (3 mm) thick. It's really time consuming, but it's a beautiful marmalade.

Kumquat marmalade with chamomile Citrus

Makes about 7 half-pint jars

INGREDIENTS

1,362 g (3 lb)	**kumquats**
10 g (¼ cup)	**fresh chamomile,** or 2 Tbsp dried chamomile flowers
1,600 g (8 cups)	**sugar** (160% of the weight of sliced kumquats)
90 g (6 Tbsp)	**lemon juice** (9% of of the weight of sliced kumquats)
776 g (3¼ cups)	**reserved kumquat** soaking liquid (yielded during the process) (78% of the weight of sliced kumquats)

Day 1 Wash the kumquats. Slice off the stem and blossom ends and set aside. Continue to slice the remaining fruit from one side of each kumquat until you hit seeds and then slice from the other side until you hit seeds. Set the middle aside. Repeat for all of the kumquats.

Using your thumb, pop out the pulp and seeds from the middle sections and set aside. Continue to slice the middle pieces into thin circles.

Put the ends along with the pulp and seeds from the middle sections in a cheesecloth sachet tied with kitchen string. Put the chamomile in a separate cheesecloth sachet or tea bag.

You should have 1,000 g kumquat slices. If you have more or less, you can figure out the amount of sugar, kumquat soaking liquid, and lemon juice you will need by using the following formula:

Grams of kumquat slices × 1.60 = grams of sugar
Grams of kumquat slices × 0.78 = grams of kumquat soaking liquid
Grams of kumquat slices × 0.09 = grams of lemon juice

Put the sliced kumquats, pulp and seed sachet, chamomile sachet, and 1,652 g (7 cups) water in a 4-quart (4 L) container. Cover and leave out on the counter overnight.

Day 2 Prepare your plate test by putting a few saucers in the freezer.

Line a fine-mesh strainer with cheesecloth and set it over a bowl so that you can reserve the liquid. Drain the kumquats and set the kumquats and liquid aside. You should have 775 g (3¼ cups) liquid. If necessary, add water or discard liquid to reach that amount.

Heat the oven to 300°F (150°C). Pour the sugar into a baking dish and warm in the oven for 10 minutes.

Combine the warm sugar, kumquat slices, pulp and seed sachet, chamomile sachet, soaking liquid, and lemon juice in a jamming pot. Cook over high heat, stirring with a heat-resistant spatula to prevent scorching.

At first it will bubble gently. As the bubbles get more vigorous it will start foaming. Skim off any scum with a spider or fine-mesh skimmer. Dip the spider into a bowl of water and give it a shake between skims to keep it clean. Cook until the bubbles get smaller, the marmalade darkens a shade in color, and the temperature reaches 221°F (105°C), 35 to 40 minutes. When the marmalade is close to being set (a few degrees before 221°F), remove from the heat. Remove the cheesecloth sachets with tongs, squeezing the bags over the pot to extract any liquid. Discard the sachets and give the jam a stir. This is a good time to perform a plate test.

Spoon a little of the marmalade gel onto a frozen saucer. Put the plate back in the freezer for 1 minute, then slide a finger through the marmalade. It's done when it parts and the marmalade at the top of your finger furrows like a brow. You should then be able to remove your finger and see a strip of clean saucer. If it isn't set, return the pot to the heat, stir constantly, and test again after 1 to 2 minutes.

To Sqirl away your marmalade, see pages 16–21.

KUMQUAT-MANDARINQUAT-LIMEQUAT MARMALADE

On one of my first visits to Rancho del Sol Organics, citrus farmer Linda Zaiser gave me all these 'quats—three varieties. Like the kumquat-chamomile marmalade on page 236, this recipe takes time and attention and a lot of deseeding. It's beautiful because of all the different sizes and colors. There are a lot of components to this marmalade and a couple of processing techniques (sliced and "shredded"), a good way to really get to know your citrus—and it's a little trickier trying to figure out a formula for making adjustments. Maybe have a few extra 'quats around to make sure you have the amount of cut fruit called for in the recipe.

Kumquat-mandarinquat-limequat marmalade Citrus

Makes about 8 half-pint jars

INGREDIENTS

510 g (1 lb 2 oz)	**kumquats**
340 g (11 oz)	**limequats**
510 g (1 lb 2 oz)	**mandarinquats**
1,350 g (6¾ cups)	**sugar** (146% of the weight of sliced citrus)
45 g (3 Tbsp)	**lemon juice** (5% of the weight of sliced citrus)
1,180 g (about 5 cups)	**reserved citrus** soaking liquid (yielded during the process) (128% of the weight of sliced citrus)

Day 1 Rinse the kumquats, limequats, and mandarinquats. Cut the kumquats and limequats: Slice off the stem and blossom ends and set them aside.

Continue to slice the remaining fruit from one side of each citrus until you hit seeds and then slice from the other side until you hit seeds. Set the middle sections aside. Repeat for all of the citrus.

Using your thumb, pop out the pulp and seeds from the middle sections and set aside. Continue to slice the middle section into thin (⅛-inch/3 mm) circles. Put the citrus ends and the pulp and seeds from the middle sections in a cheesecloth sachet tied with kitchen string.

Put the sliced kumquats and limequats, cheesecloth sachet, and 710 g (3 cups) water in a 2-quart (2 L) container. Cover and set aside to leave out overnight.

Cut the mandarinquats in half crosswise and juice them, being careful not to tear the peels (these go into your marmalade). Set the juice aside. Pull out the membrane, pulp, and seeds and put them in a cheesecloth sachet.

Slice the peels into thin (⅛-inch/3 mm) strips and put them in a 2-quart (2 L) container along with the mandarinquat juice, cheesecloth sachet, and 600 g (2½ cups) water. Cover and leave out on the counter overnight.

Day 2 Prepare your plate test by putting a few saucers in the freezer.

Strain the liquid from the kumquats and limequats into a pot and set the sliced fruit and cheesecloth sachet aside. Add the mandarinquats and their liquid to the pot, setting aside the cheesecloth sachet. Bring to a boil. Boil for 30 seconds and remove from the heat.

Heat the oven to 300°F (150°C). Pour the sugar into a baking dish and warm in the oven for 10 minutes.

Combine the warm sugar, citrus slices, cheesecloth sachet, lemon juice, and cooking liquid in a jamming pot. Cook over high heat, stirring with a heatproof spatula to prevent scorching.

At first, it will bubble gently. As the bubbles get more vigorous it will start foaming. Use a spider or fine-mesh skimmer to skim off any scum. Dip the spider into a bowl of water and give it a shake to clean between skims. Cook until the bubbles get smaller, the marmalade is a shade deeper in color, and the temperature reaches 221°F (105°C), 25 to 30 minutes. When the marmalade is close to being set (a few degrees before 221°F), remove from the heat. Remove the cheesecloth sachet with tongs, squeezing the bag over the pot to extract any liquid. Discard the sachet and give the jam a stir. This is a good time for a plate test.

Spoon a little of the marmalade gel onto a frozen saucer. Put the plate back in the freezer for 1 minute, then slide a finger through the marmalade. It's done when it parts and the marmalade at the top of your finger furrows like a brow. You should then be able to remove your finger and see a strip of clean saucer. If it isn't set, return the pot to the heat, stir constantly, and test again after 1 to 2 minutes.

To Sqirl away your marmalade see pages 16–21.

RANGPUR LIME–MANDARIN MARMALADE

Rangpur lime is a hybrid of citron and mandarin (and it looks a lot like a mandarin). The fruit is very tart, and the rind and juice have a bright spicy flavor, which means they're just right for marmalades. This is the only marmalade we make where we use the fruit segments, which ultimately find themselves delicately suspended in the jelly. It's almost too pretty to eat.

Makes 8 half-pint jars

INGREDIENTS

600 g (1 lb 5 oz)	**mandarins**
400 g (14 oz)	**Rangpur limes**
1,250 g (6¼ cups)	**sugar** (125% of the weight of mandarins plus Rangpur limes)
45 g (3 Tbsp)	**lemon juice** (5% of the weight of mandarins plus Rangpur limes)
711 g (2¾ cups plus 1½ Tbsp)	**blood orange pectin** (page 214) (75% of the weight of mandarins plus Rangpur limes)

Prepare your plate test by putting a few saucers in the freezer.

Peel the mandarins and break up the segments. Cut the segments in half, removing the seeds as you go (setting them aside). Discard the peel and set the segments aside. (You should have about 438 g peeled and deseeded segments.)

Cut the Rangpur limes crosswise and juice them. Set the juice aside. (You should have about 157 g juice.) Scrape out the membrane, pulp, and seeds using a spoon. Or do this with your hands—invert the peel and from the center remove the membrane and pulp. Set the peels aside. (You should have 95 g Rangpur lime peels.) Put the membrane, pulp, and all of your seeds in a food processor and pulse until the membranes are finely chopped. Transfer to a cheesecloth sack tied with kitchen string and set aside.

Quarter the peels by cutting the halves lengthwise. Stack a few of the quartered peels at a time and slice them crosswise into very thin (2 mm) strips. Put the strips and cheesecloth sack into a pot.

Add enough water to the lime juice so that you have 1½ cups and pour it over the strips of peel. Bring to a boil, then simmer for 5 minutes to soften the rind. Remove from the heat.

Heat the oven to 300°F (150°C). Pour the sugar into a baking dish and warm for 10 minutes.

Combine the lime peels and their poaching liquid in a jamming pot along with the mandarin segments, cheesecloth sack, warmed sugar, lemon juice, and blood orange pectin over high heat. Stir with a heatproof spatula as your marmalade cooks. It initially will bubble gently. As it bubbles more vigorously it will start foaming (like foam on top of a soda just poured from a can). Skim off any scum or seeds with a spider or fine-mesh skimmer. Dip the spider into a large bowl of water and give it a shake to clean between skims. Cook until the bubbles get smaller, the marmalade looks a shade deeper in color, and the temperature nears 221°F (105°C), about 25 minutes. A few degrees before the marmalade reaches 221°F, remove from the heat. Remove the cheesecloth sachet with tongs, squeezing the bag over the pot to extract any liquid. Discard the sachet and give the jam a stir. This is a good time to perform a plate test.

Spoon a little of the marmalade gel onto a frozen saucer. Put the plate back in the freezer for 1 minute, then slide a finger through the marmalade. It's done when it parts and the jelly at the top of your finger furrows like a brow. You should then be able to remove your finger and see a strip of clean saucer. If it isn't set, return the pot to the heat, stir constantly, and test again after 1 to 2 minutes.

To Sqirl away your marmalade, see pages 16–21.

Rangpur lime–mandarin marmalade Citrus

YUZU MARMALADE WITH HONEY

Floral yuzu with floral honey just makes sense. This marmalade is different from most of the other marmalades in this chapter because you're using the pulp, which gives it a great texture.

Yuzu marmalade with honey Citrus

Makes 6 to 8 half-pint jars

INGREDIENTS

1,589 g (3 lb 8 oz)	**yuzu**
731 g (3⅔ cups)	**sugar** [56% of the weight of blanched yuzu peel plus pulp]
292 g (¾ cup plus 2 Tbsp)	**honey** [23% of the weight of blanched yuzu peel plus pulp]
160 g (⅔ cup)	**yuzu juice** (yielded during the process) [12% of the weight of blanched yuzu peel plus pulp]
75 g (5 Tbsp)	**lemon juice** [5% of the weight of blanched yuzu peel plus pulp]

Note: If you don't have any honey, you can use all sugar for this recipe—the same amount by weight.

Cut the yuzu into quarters lengthwise, removing the seeds as you go—they have a lot of seeds! Take the time to pick out as many as you can during this step. Collect any juice released during this process. Discard the seeds.

Juice the quartered yuzu over a strainer to remove any remaining seeds. Sadly it's not as much juice as you'd expect. Make sure to maintain the shape of the peels when juicing (try not to tear or break them, because they will be used in the marmalade). Set the juice aside.

Pull out the membrane and pulp from each quartered yuzu. Put the membranes and pulp in a medium pot with enough water to cover. Bring to a boil, then simmer for 10 minutes to soften. Drain and discard the liquid. Let the membranes cool slightly, then roughly chop them. Set aside.

Cut the yuzu peels (you can stack a few at a time) lengthwise into very thin (2 mm) strips. Put the peels in a large pot. Add enough water to cover the peels and bring to a boil, then simmer for 10 minutes. Remove from the heat and drain, discarding the water. Repeat this step one more time. (This helps soften the peels and removes bitterness.) Set the blanched peels aside.

You should have 1,295 g blanched yuzu peel plus pulp. If you have more or less, you can figure out how much sugar, honey, yuzu juice, and lemon juice you need with the following formula:

Grams of blanched yuzu peel plus pulp × 0.56 = grams of sugar
Grams of blanched yuzu peel plus pulp × 0.23 = grams of honey
Grams of blanched yuzu peel plus pulp × 0.12 = grams of yuzu juice
Grams of blanched yuzu peel plus pulp × 0.05 = grams of lemon juice

Prepare your plate test by putting a few saucers in the freezer.

Heat the oven to 300°F (150°C). Pour the sugar into a baking dish and warm in the oven for 10 minutes.

Combine the warm sugar, honey, yuzu peel, pulp, yuzu juice, and lemon juice in a jamming pot. Cook over high heat, stirring with a heatproof spatula to prevent scorching. At first it will bubble gently. As it bubbles more vigorously it will start foaming. Skim off any scum or seeds with a spider or fine-mesh skimmer. Dip the spider into a bowl of water and give it a shake to clean it between skims. Cook until the bubbles get smaller, the marmalade is a darker shade of golden, and the temperature reaches 221°F (105°C), 15 to 20 minutes. A few degrees before the marmalade reaches 221°F, remove from the heat and perform a plate test.

Spoon a little of the marmalade gel onto a frozen saucer. Put the plate back in the freezer for 1 minute, then slide a finger through the marmalade. It's done when it parts and the marmalade at the top of your finger furrows like a brow. You should then be able to remove your finger and see a strip of clean saucer. If it isn't set, return to the heat, stir frequently, and test again after 1 to 3 minutes.

To Sqirl away your marmalade, see pages 16–21.

Variation: Yuzu marmalade with shiso

Put 5 shiso leaves in a sachet of cheesecloth tied with kitchen string and add this to the jamming pot along with the yuzu, sugar, honey, and lemon juice. Proceed with the recipe as directed. Remove the sachet of shiso with a pair of tongs as the marmalade nears setting. Proceed with the rest of the recipe above.

MEYER LEMON–KIWI MARMALADE

This marmalade's just fun. It's like talking to your gorgeous friend who's also wildly intelligent. A total knockout. Delicious. The kiwi here has a confetti effect—and it adds pectin, too.

Meyer lemon–kiwi marmalade Citrus

Makes about 9 half-pint jars

INGREDIENTS

1,475 g (3 lb 4 oz)	**Meyer lemons**
1,475 g (3 lb 4 oz)	**kiwis**
1,500 g (7½ cups)	**sugar** (73% of the weight of cooked lemon triangles plus sliced kiwis)
45 g (3 Tbsp)	**Meyer lemon juice** (2% of the weight of blanched lemon triangles plus sliced kiwis)
90 g (6 Tbsp)	**regular lemon juice** (4% of the weight of blanched lemon triangles plus sliced kiwis)

Day 1 Wash the Meyer lemons. Cut off the stem and blossom ends and set them aside. Cut the lemons into quarters lengthwise. Cut each quarter crosswise into thin (⅛ inch/3 mm) slices, creating triangles, removing any seeds as you go. Put the seeds and ends in a cheesecloth sachet tied with kitchen string.

Put the lemon triangles, sachet of seeds and ends, and 945 g (4 cups) water in a 4-quart (4 L) container. Cover and leave out on the counter overnight.

Day 2 Prepare your plate test by putting a few saucers in the freezer.

Line a fine-mesh strainer with cheesecloth and set it over a large pot. Pour the contents of the container into the strainer and set the drained triangles aside.

Bring the liquid to a boil. Add the triangles to the pot and boil until soft, 15 minutes. Remove from the heat.

Drain and discard the liquid, reserving the lemon triangles. Make sure to fully drain so that there's as little liquid as possible. You should have 910 g lemon triangles. Prepare the kiwis: Cut off the stem and blossom ends of the kiwis. Using a peeler, remove the kiwi peels and discard. Cut the fruit lengthwise into quarters and then crosswise into 5 mm pieces. You should have 1,180 g sliced kiwi.

If you have more or less than 2,090 g cooked lemon triangles plus sliced kiwi, you can figure out the amount of sugar, Meyer lemon juice, and regular lemon juice you need with the following formula:

Grams of cooked lemon triangles
plus sliced kiwi × 0.73 = grams of sugar
Grams of cooked lemon triangles
plus sliced kiwi × 0.02 = grams of Meyer lemon juice
Grams of cooked lemon triangles plus
sliced kiwi × 0.04 = grams of lemon juice

Combine the lemon triangles, sliced kiwi, cheesecloth sachet, warmed sugar, and lemon juices in a jamming pot. Cook over high heat, stirring occasionally with a heatproof spatula. At first, it will bubble gently. As it bubbles more vigorously it will start foaming. Skim off any scum or seeds with a spider or fine-mesh skimmer. Dip the spider into a bowl of water and give it a shake to clean between skims. Cook until the bubbles get smaller, the marmalade turns one shade darker in color, and the temperature reaches 216°F (103°C), 20 to 25 minutes. Remove from the heat. Remove the cheesecloth sachet with tongs, squeezing the bag over the pot to extract any liquid. Discard the sachet and give the jam a stir. This is a good time to perform a plate test.

Spoon a little of the marmalade onto a frozen saucer. Put the plate back in the freezer for 1 minute, then slide a finger through the marmalade. It's done when it parts and the marmalade at the top of your finger furrows like a brow. You should then be able to remove your finger and see a strip of clean saucer. If it isn't set, return to the heat, stir constantly, and test again after 1 to 2 minutes.

To Sqirl away your marmalade, see pages 16–21.

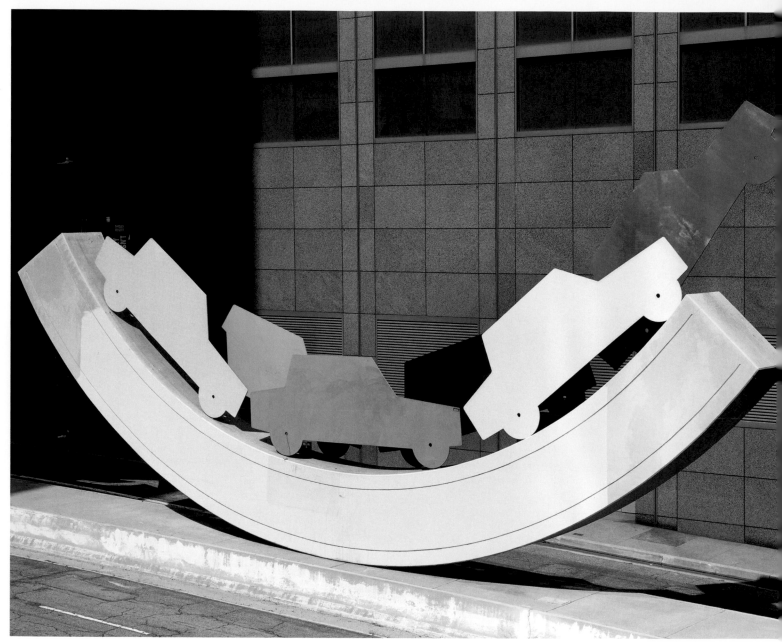

Lloyd Hamrol, Uptown Rocker, Bunker Hill, Los Angeles

Retracing Erwin Wurm with lemons, downtown Los Angeles

Citrus

CANDIED POMELO RIND

Pomelo and grapefruit make the bitterest marmalades. Just ask the internet. Save yourself: Eat the fruit, use the rind for candying.

Candied pomelo rind Citrus

You can substitute grapefruit or other citrus for the pomelo. For oranges, blanch the peels only twice. Citric acid adds bright tartness.

Makes about 28 pieces

INGREDIENTS

815 g (1 lb 13 oz)	**pomelo**
600 g (3 cups)	**granulated sugar**
¼ tsp	**cream of tartar**
50 g (¼ cup)	**superfine sugar**
½ tsp	**citric acid (optional)**

Cut the pomelo in half crosswise and juice it. Save the juice for another use (or you could drink it). Using a spoon, scoop out the membranes and white pith and discard. Pomelos have a very thick pith, but try to scoop out as much as possible so that you have only a smooth, thin layer of pith connected to the peel.

Cut the peel halves lengthwise into ½-inch (12 mm) slices. If there is still excess pith, you can use a sharp knife to cut off any excess.

Put the pomelo peel slices in a small saucepan and cover with cold water. Bring to a boil, then reduce to a simmer and cook for 10 minutes. Drain and repeat two more times.

Return the pomelo peel slices to the saucepan and cover with water. Bring to a boil and then simmer until tender, 30 to 35 minutes. Drain, discarding the liquid.

Put the granulated sugar and 708 g (3 cups) water in a saucepan and bring to a boil without stirring. Reduce to a simmer and add the cream of tartar and pomelo slices. Cook until translucent and the temperature of the syrup reaches 221°F (105°C), 40 to 45 minutes.

Line a baking sheet with parchment paper or a Silpat. Place a cooling rack on top of the baking sheet and brush the rack with oil. Using a slotted spoon, remove the candied peels from the syrup and transfer to the oiled cooling rack. Reserve the syrup for another use (such as for the citrus sponge cake on page 252). Leave the candied peels out to dry until they are still tacky but no longer dripping, about 12 hours.

Combine the superfine sugar and citric acid (if using) in a large bowl. Once the peels are dry but still tacky, toss them in the sugar. Store in an airtight container for up to 1 month.

This can be made with all sorts of juices. I've used Rangpur lime. Meyer lemon is great. Blood orange, too. We use citrus curd in an atypical way at Sqirl—as a frosting for cake instead of buttercream. As you may have read before (page 190), I love curd. My grandmother was British, so I grew up in a house of going to tea services and eating lots of scones with clotted cream and curd. And that curd has to be really acidic. That's how Essie would have wanted it.

Makes 610 g (2½ cups)

INGREDIENTS

200 g (1 cup)	**sugar**
2	**whole large eggs**
6	**egg yolks**
240 g (1 cup)	**citrus juice**
114 g (½ cup/1 stick)	**unsalted butter, cubed and softened**
¼ tsp	**salt**
3 Tbsp	**grated citrus zest**

In a medium heatproof bowl, whisk together the sugar, whole eggs, and egg yolks until smooth. Whisk in the citrus juice until combined.

Put the bowl over a pot of lightly simmering water. I like to cook it low and slow, which takes a while but doesn't require any babysitting. Leave it on the water bath over low heat at a low simmer, whisking occasionally, until the temperature reaches about 160°F (71°C) and it's about the consistency of sour cream, 30 to 40 minutes. Remove from the heat.

Whisk in the butter a couple cubes at a time until incorporated. Whisk in the salt and zest. Store in the refrigerator with plastic wrap placed directly onto the curd to prevent a skin from forming for up to 1 week.

Citrus curd Citrus

Citrus sponge cake with citrus curd Citrus

If you don't have candied citrus peel, you can substitute extra zest for flavor. And instead of using the leftover syrup from candied citrus as your soak, dissolve 150 g (¾ cup) sugar in 150 g (½ cup plus 2 tsp) hot water for a 1:1 simple syrup; add the grated zest of 2 or 3 citrus (any combination of orange, lemon, yuzu, and grapefruit).

Makes 1 (10-inch/25 cm) cake

INGREDIENTS

520 g (2¼ cups/4½ sticks)	**butter**
200 g (¾ cup plus 4 tsp)	**milk**
8	**large eggs**
700 g (3½ cups)	**sugar**
1 tsp	**vanilla paste**
320 g (2½ cups)	**all-purpose flour**
320 g (2½ cups)	**whole-wheat flour** (we use Grist & Toll Sonora)
4 tsp	**baking powder**
1 Tbsp	**salt**
½ tsp	**ground cardamom**
	Grated zest of 6 lemons (or yuzu)
	Grated zest of 4 limes
	Grated zest of 6 oranges (or 4 grapefruit)
	Juice of 2 oranges or 4 lemons
208 g (1⅓ cups)	**candied citrus** (page 248)
240 g (1 cup)	**heavy cream**
488 g (2 cups)	**citrus curd** (page 250)
About 120 g (½ cup)	**reserved syrup from candied citrus** (page 248)
	Dehydrated citrus slices, fresh berries, or poppy seeds for garnish

Heat the oven to 350°F (175°C). Prepare a 10-inch (25 cm) round cake pan by spraying it with vegetable oil spray or greasing it with butter and lining the bottom with parchment paper.

Heat the butter and milk in a saucepan over medium heat until the butter has melted. Set aside and let cool to room temperature.

In the bowl of a stand mixer fitted with the whisk attachment, whisk the eggs, sugar, and vanilla paste until light and fluffy. Add the milk and butter mixture and mix thoroughly.

Sift the flours, baking powder, salt, and cardamom into a large bowl. Fold the flour mixture into the egg mixture until incorporated. Gently stir in the zests, orange juice, and candied citrus.

Pour the batter into the prepared cake pan and bake until a cake tester or skewer inserted in the center comes out clean, about 30 minutes. Let cool completely.

Make a citrus curd Bavarian cream for the top layer of the cake: Whip the cream with a hand mixer or in the bowl of a standing mixer until soft peaks form. Put 244 g (1 cup) of the curd in a bowl and fold in the whipped cream. Set aside.

Invert the cake and remove the pan and parchment paper. With a serrated knife, trim the top of the cake just enough so that there is a mostly flat surface. Carefully split the cake in half horizontally.

Thoroughly brush the cut side of the bottom layer with 3 to 4 Tbsp of the syrup. Top with about 244 g (1 cup) of the citrus curd and use a spatula to spread it to the edges (it shouldn't be spilling out beyond the edges). Place the second cake layer on top of the first. Brush with 3 to 4 Tbsp syrup. Top with the citrus curd Bavarian cream. Garnish as desired with dehydrated citrus slices, berries, or a sprinkling of poppy seeds. Serve immediately.

I wanted this book to end like a great meal—with a cup of coffee and the crunch of biscotti.

Makes 21 biscotti

INGREDIENTS

344 g (2¾ cups)	**all-purpose flour,** sifted
250 g (1¼ cups)	**sugar,** plus more for sprinkling
70 g (½ cup)	**whole almonds,** toasted and roughly chopped
2 tsp	**toasted fennel seeds**
1½ tsp	**baking powder**
½ tsp	**salt**
	Finely grated zest of 1 orange
114 g (½ cup/1 stick)	**unsalted butter,** softened and cubed
113 g (¾ cup)	**chopped candied pomelo rinds** (page 248)
2	**whole large eggs, at room temperature**
½ tsp	**vanilla extract**
1 Tbsp	**orange liqueur**
1	**egg white,** lightly beaten

Mix the flour, sugar, almonds, fennel seeds, baking powder, salt, and orange zest in the bowl of a mixer fitted with the paddle attachment.

Add the butter and mix on low speed until the mixture has a wet sand consistency, about 2 minutes. Add the candied rinds and mix on low just until incorporated.

In a separate bowl, whisk together the eggs, vanilla, and orange liqueur, then pour this into the flour mixture. Mix on low speed until incorporated.

Transfer the dough to a lightly floured piece of parchment paper and transfer to a baking sheet. Shape the dough into a flat-topped log, 4 inches (10 cm) wide, 16 inches (40.5 cm) long, and ½ inch (12 mm) thick. Use a rolling pin to smooth out the top of the dough.

Cover with plastic wrap and put the log of dough in the refrigerator to rest for 30 minutes.

Heat the oven to 325°F (165°C).

Remove the plastic wrap and brush the dough with egg white and sprinkle generously with sugar. Bake until light brown and still slightly soft, 40 minutes. Let cool for 20 minutes. Leave the oven on.

Using a serrated knife, cut the log crosswise into slices ½ inch (12 mm) thick. Set a cooling rack on a sheet pan. Place the slices on the rack and return to the 325°F (165°C) oven. Bake until golden brown and almost firm to the touch, 15 to 20 minutes, flipping each biscotti after 10 minutes.

Let cool before serving. You can keep these in a covered container at room temperature for up to 2 weeks. Hopefully they won't last long.

Biscotti with almonds and candied pomelo Citrus

Editor: Holly Dolce
Designer: Scott Barry
Production Managers: Rebecca Westall and
Denise LaCongo

Library of Congress Control Number:
2018945580

ISBN: 978-1-4197-3533-2
eISBN: 978-1-68335-501-4

Text copyright © 2020 Jessica Koslow
Photographs copyright © 2020 Scott Barry
Cover © 2020 Abrams

Printed and bound in China
10 9 8 7 6 5 4 3 2 1

Abrams books are available at special discounts
when purchased in quantity for premiums
and promotions as well as fundraising or
educational use. Special editions can also be
created to specification. For details, contact
specialsales@abramsbooks.com or the address
below.

Abrams® is a registered trademark
of Harry N. Abrams, Inc.

ABRAMS The Art of Books
195 Broadway, New York, NY 10007
abramsbooks.com